6740388
5680569

COME WALK WITH ME

FOREWORD BY BILLY AND RUTH GRAHAM

A STORY OF COMPASSIONATE LOVE AND
RESPECT BETWEEN A FATHER AND HIS SON

COME WALK WITH ME

MELVIN CHEATHAM, M.D.

WITH MARK CUTSHALL

AFTERWORD BY FRANKLIN GRAHAM

THOMAS NELSON PUBLISHERS
Nashville

Published in Nashville, Tennessee, by Thomas Nelson, Inc.

Scripture quotations designated NKJV are from The Holy Bible: New King James Version, © 1982 by Thomas Nelson, Inc., Nashville, Tennessee.

Library of Congress Cataloging-in-Publication Data

Cheatham, Melvin L.
    Come walk with me / Melvin L. Cheatham, with Mark Cut-shall.
        p. cm.
    ISBN 0-8407-4249-5 (pbk.) 0-7852-8291-2 (cb)
    1. Cheatham Melvin L. 2. Missionaries, Medical—Kenya—Biography. 3. Cheborge, Stanley. I. Cutshall, Mark. II. Title.
R722.32.C39A3   1993
610.69'5–dc20   93-4069
                                                                  CIP

Printed in the United States of America

3 4 5 6 7 8 9 BVG 02 01 00 99 98 97

DEDICATION

Come Walk with Me is dedicated to the many Christian servants who seek out the sick, the hungry, the suffering, the forgotten, and minister to them in the name of Jesus Christ. The names of some of these people are found within the pages of this book. Countless others around the world will not be known, as they continue their lives of giving.

Special words of dedication are given to Jane Jones, editor of this project. Jane's heart was deeply touched by the story of Stanley Cheborge. Shortly after editing my manuscript, Jane died of an inoperable brain tumor.

To my mother, who read Bible stories to me as a child, and to my father, who was my friend and inspiration, I owe untold thanks.

To my wife, Sylvia, who has been my partner in all of life, and courageously so in times of service with World Medical Mission; and to our children, who have supported all our efforts, I dedicate this book.

Finally, I give God the glory for the lives portrayed in this book, for the wonder of life, for His love and blessings, and for those who answer the call of Christ to "Come Walk with Me."

Melvin L. Cheatham, M.D.

FOREWORD

Come Walk with Me will challenge and inspire you. It will grip, inform, and entertain you. And when you are finished reading, you will be changed. You'll say, "Here I am, Lord. Do with me whatever You want." And He will. Then you'll know a joy and a fulfilling you've never experienced before.

This is a story of medical missions and the untiring service of Christians who have committed their lives to helping others. But it is more than that. It is the story of lives—lives that know sorrow and happiness, illness and health, death and new life. It is the story of people who share the Good News of Jesus Christ wherever they go.

Missionary medicine has always had a special place in our hearts. Dr. L. Nelson Bell, Ruth's father, served as a medical missionary in China for twenty-five years, and he had great influence on our lives. Knowing Mel and Sylvia Cheatham as they serve with our son, Franklin, in the work of Samaritan's Purse and World Medical Mission has enriched us, too.

In this book the Cheathams open their hearts to tell you the story of the Lord's working through His servants. They share with you a glimpse of life in the African bush, and the compassionate, loving respect of a son for his father and a father for his son. *Come Walk with Me* will move and stimulate you. It will bring tears to your eyes, and you won't be able to put it down.

May its message encourage you to go out and love your neighbors, to feel greater compassion for those who suffer, and to do what you can to care for the sick.

Won't you join hands with us and other Christians around the world as we seek to serve in our Lord's name? Come, we'll walk together.

—Billy and Ruth Graham

ONE

The smell of sickness hung in the air at Tenwek Hospital. It greeted me like a familiar companion on a day that has never faded from my memory. In fact what happened that morning changed my life forever, both as a physician and as a follower of the Great Physician.

Come back with me and you will begin to understand.

Returning in my memory to the small operating room of the 250-bed hospital in western Kenya is like looking through a mental scrapbook and finding a favorite photograph. The images are still sharp and clear—the heavy overhead surgical lights, the tired, ancient operating table, the gracious Kenyan nurses. A single, sparsely filled cabinet stands against the wall, and the anesthesia machine looks old enough to be an antique. I reach to pick up the photograph and my memories come to life, again.

My translucent rubber gloves touched his black skin. Preparation for the surgery was almost complete. Anesthesia would soon bring a complete loss of feeling from his lower rib cage to his toes. A gray wool Kenyan blanket elevated his hips, freeing his abdomen so he could breathe more easily.

The anticipation that always precedes surgery began to build inside me like a slow fire. The mounting emotion was no different from the feelings that had preceded the thousands of other surgeries I had performed back home in California. The difference was that I was in Kenya, more than 10,000 miles from home. I was in a mission hospital, a facility that provided the only medical care available in a large area that was home to 300,000 Kenyan natives. I was a medical mission volunteer.

Less than forty-eight hours before, my plane had touched down on the grassy earth of East Africa. Now I was looking down at a twenty-six-year-old Kipsigis tribesman named Stanley and preparing to operate on his spine. And I was as unaware as he was of what the next few hours would bring.

I held the surgical knife firmly in my right hand and placed the blade against the skin over his lower spine. Then I drew the edge downward. The incision created a small chasm. After a moment the bleeding began.

Short bursts of electric fire from the electrocautery sealed each small blood vessel as it erupted, and I progressively deepened the incision until I could feel his spine. Then I stripped and separated the muscles from their attachments to the bone. Below this lay the cause of Stanley's pain.

I needed to see the problem, for the facilities of Tenwek Hospital were unable to provide the kind of information I was accustomed to having before surgery. I had a hunch or two, but I really didn't know what I would find.

Biting away the bone, I exposed the spinal cord sac. Through its bluish-gray transparency I could see the spinal nerves floating in the fluid. For a moment I saw the intersection of a doctor's career and a young man's life, and I wondered why Africa? And why Mel Cheatham?

Back home in Ventura, California, I used an operating microscope for neurosurgery. This morning, in the first neurosurgery I performed at Tenwek, I had to rely on surgical magnifying glasses. They fit snugly around my head, and I could see things two and one-half times as large as they were in real life. Without this improved vision, successful surgery would be impossible. At least now, there was some hope.

I was in my fiftieth year when Tenwek Hospital became a significant part of my world. I thought I could see life clearly, but this young Kipsigis tribesman helped me see with new eyes. His name was Stanley Cheborge, and I'll never forget him.

I looked down at him and thought of the pain he would feel waking up. I thought of the night before when I first met him. Dr. Bob Wesche, a missionary surgeon from Michigan, and I had worked all afternoon performing general surgeries, one right after the other. In the middle of an operation, Dr. Marty Graber, a visiting physician from Indiana, came into the room and said, "Stanley's here, and he's waiting to see you." Bob and I finished the operation, and within minutes I was standing in the doorway of a small cubicle bathed in dim light. I could see a tall, thin black man lying on a bed. He was supporting his upper torso on one elbow. And a broad grin was spread across his face. "Welcome, my name is Stanley! You must be Dr. Cheatham. I'm sure you are very weary from your long journey. Please, come in and sit down."

Stanley Cheborge was not like other patients. Whatever the problem, most people naturally begin to talk about their condition—how they feel, how they slept the night before, how they want to go home from the hospital. But with Stanley there was no self-pity, no longing for attention, and no mention of his illness. Instead, he wanted to know what *I* was feeling. His interest was genuine and deep. His words resonated warmth. His voice was alive. Within a few moments I observed a depth of character I've seen in only a few other people in my life.

After Stanley had greeted me, he greeted Bob Wesche. For the next several minutes they talked effortlessly. I stood on the fringe of their conversation, listening in without trying.

"Yes, this is Dr. Cheatham," Bob said. "He is the neurosurgeon who will be able to explain the pain that keeps throbbing in your lower back and keeps radiating down your lower leg."

"I know God has brought Dr. Cheatham to take away my pain and restore me to health," Stanley said. There was total confidence in his voice. Would I, the surgeon, speak with as much confidence after I cut to the core of his pain and saw a fragile, human condition staring back?

I looked over this young man and wondered what it would be like to lose a leg. Had I known him better, I could have asked Stanley. What I had already learned about him only whetted my desire to know more.

When Stanley was only six, he began herding his family's sheep, cattle, and goats. Every day he faced the threat of hungry, wild animals and raiding Maasai tribesmen. In the teeth of these hazards, Stanley learned to survive. Avoiding danger on a daily basis was not so much a matter of courage as it was a necessity of life.

This young man dreamed of becoming a great runner. By the time he was fourteen, Stanley stood six feet tall. He was blessed with long, muscular legs, and he loved to race across the vast open grasslands of western Kenya. He could outrun almost every opponent.

One day while running, Stanley thought he had pulled a muscle. At first, he had a dull ache in his left knee. Gradually, the pain grew.

"Perhaps exercise will help," he thought. He tried racing across the savannah through the short new grass brought to life by early summer rains. He dodged zebra, giraffe, and impala, running in a wide circle to stay out of the territorial hunt of lions.

The soles of his feet, hardened by years of going barefoot, were as thick as leather. Unlike his left knee, they were numb to pain. Over the next month, the pain in his knee grew worse until almost every stride was agonizing. Then, on the soccer field at school, the leg snapped, and the fall twisted Stanley to the ground. His hands clenched tightly into an angry ball. And he screamed.

There were tears. For a young, confident athlete, the injury was an embarrassing admission of weakness, even failure. His own body had broken his pride. He was carried to his family's hut, and there he braced himself for the future. The uncertainty lasted three days. When tribal medicine didn't relieve his pain, Stanley's family carried him twenty miles to Tenwek Hospital. There Dr. Ernie Steury, a missionary doctor from Berne, Indiana, told Stanley and his family there was evidence of a tumor that had been slowly eating away at the bone below the knee. The stress of running had caused the diseased bone to break. To save Stanley's life, Dr. Steury amputated Stanley's left leg.

I could stop here and explain how this single event altered Stanley's life. But you will find out soon enough. For now you need only to imagine this proud Kipsigis tribesman returning home to his village as a cripple, unable to stand or walk without help, and being watched intensely by forty or so well-wishers.

What silent doubts he must have carried inside himself. "Will I be accepted by my friends?" "Will I be an outcast now?" "Will people be able to take their eyes off this amputation stump and see *me*?"

Stanley was forced to face being totally dependent on his family and friends. Someone had fashioned a sturdy tree limb into a pole about six feet long and two inches thick. Using it for support, Stanley was able to stand on his right leg and propel himself along in a swinging motion by placing the pole ahead, then hopping forward on his right foot. Imagine the world champion in the 100 meter dash reduced to hobbling with a stick. This is the picture of Stanley Cheborge standing alone with his fractured pride.

He began to venture out of the family compound and visit friends and acquaintances. No longer swift of foot, he trudged along in an awkward dance, lunging then halting—steadied by one pole and then one leg.

It took about six weeks for the amputation stump to heal. Then Dr. Steury located a crudely made crutch. But the hope of walking proved artificial. Stanley found the crutch painful and awkward. The whole tragedy might not have touched me so powerfully, except for one thing. Stanley had started a Sunday school class for some small children at Aisaik Primary School. In spite of his pain, he was already reaching out to others.

After one year of secondary school at Kabungut, he was accepted at Tenwek School where he could get around more easily. But that presented a new problem: Without money for a bus ride, how would he get from Tenwek to Aisaik to teach the Sunday school class? Stanley solved that problem by walking seven miles both ways once each week the entire school year so he could continue teaching the class. It meant waking up at five o'clock every Sunday morning. This gave him enough time to hobble the seven dusty, sometimes muddy, miles to Aisaik and back, all on one leg and a bent stick. He did that for a group of students who meant more to him than the inconvenience of walking for six hours.

Once I heard this story I began to understand how unusual he was.

I looked down at him on the operating table and saw the look of total calm on his face. I thought to myself, "Mel Cheatham, you have been given so much in life and yet you do so little with it. This young man has so little, and he has already done so much with his life. What can you learn from him?"

Moments before the operation began, Stanley had looked at me and said, "Dr. Cheatham, I prayed to God last night and again this morning and thanked Him for bringing you here to operate on my spine. I know that He is going to use you in healing my body. I have placed my entire trust in the Lord and I know He loves me and He will not fail me. He is always faithful. Because of this I slept well last night, and even now I am at peace."

"Stanley, it's a privilege to be here at Tenwek and to have this opportunity to try to help you," I responded. "Is there anything I can do to put your mind at ease?" As I looked at him, I realized the humor of my words. Stanley was *already* at ease. Before the words were out of my mouth, his face broke into a wide grin, revealing the gap between the slightly mottled teeth in the center of his smile.

In fact it struck me that he might have been more relaxed than I was! And it didn't make sense. Stanley was the one who would spend the morning under the scalpel, not me. Suddenly the thought of doing neurosurgery in a strange place with such limited equipment made my doubts more reasonable and my prayers more ardent.

Stanley remained still. His body numbed by the anesthesia, he was unaware of what might be found inside him. I moved the spinal fluid sac slightly and then I saw it—the abnormality I had discovered in the X-rays taken before the operation.

They had revealed that Stanley had a serious problem; a portion of his spine seemed to have been eaten away. An earlier examination showed some weakness and numbness in his leg, which confirmed an earlier suspicion of a pinched nerve. But the numbness extended further than I would expect from a pinched nerve or even a ruptured disc.

After seeing the X-ray, I had decided to perform a myelogram. This procedure involves injecting material into the lower spinal fluid sac that will outline the spine. Another X-ray would reveal if there were an abnormality. The Kenyan X-ray technician handed me several sheets of smoky film taken with Tenwek's old X-ray machine. One by one I held them up to the light, then let out a deep sigh. I saw what Stanley had been carrying for weeks, maybe months. The X-rays hinted that Stanley had cancer of the bone.

Now, only minutes into surgery, my suspicions were confirmed. A large tumor extended from the bone and displaced the spinal fluid sac. It was grayish-purple and it bled easily when I touched it with my surgical forceps. Bob Wesche was assisting me and he saw it too. I glanced across the table at Bob and his eyes spoke the disappointment we both felt. I looked over the sterile drapes that hid Stanley's face from the unkind reality at my fingertips. He was dozing, feeling nothing because of the spinal anesthesia, and unaware that his body had betrayed him again.

Sorrow swept over me. It welled up deep inside and found the corners of my eyes. Sadness such as this had struck my heart many times before when I found cancer in other patients. Except this time the emotion was more intense. Perhaps it was because after coming nearly halfway around the world to help patients at Tenwek, my efforts were being defeated with this first neurosurgery case. Or maybe it was the realization that back home, cancer patients at least received pain medication and good medical care. I knew that once Stanley returned to his village, he would have neither to rely on. Now all I could seem to do was stand by his side and feel a sense of helplessness.

"Why this man?" I wondered. And why now? How could this cancer, which had already robbed Stanley of his left leg, have remained dormant in his body for twelve years? Like facing an intruder too strong to be evicted, I wondered if anything could stop this tumor from spreading and robbing Stanley of life.

I worked quickly to remove as much of the cancerous growth as possible. I clutched a biopsy forceps and bit into the tumor to confirm the malignancy. There was heavy bleeding. I kept biting into the tumor, and as I removed more, I found more.

I glanced over at Marty Graber, who was monitoring the vital signs. He and his wife, Ann, were Stanley's special friends. Wordlessly, Marty started a blood transfusion to keep up with the blood Stanley was losing every minute. When our eyes met he looked down and slowly shook his head.

The bleeding from the tumor intensified. Without some gelfoam and thrombin, aids to help promote clotting I always had when I operated at home, it was very difficult to control the bleeding. I was beginning to be uneasy about getting it stopped, when the antiquated suction machine suddenly failed. Blood welled up in the wound and began to pour down the sterile drapes and onto the floor. I could feel my heart pounding against my ribcage and hear its urgent pulse in my head. Bob Wesche and I worked urgently in silence.

Thirty minutes must have passed. Gradually and mercifully, the bleeding slowed. Time and surgical instruments brought it under control. My muscles were tiring. Sweat was running down my face behind the lenses of my surgical glasses, but I could see enough. Portions of the tumor still remained lodged in Stanley's spine and extended deep into his body. The cancer had resisted.

I stared down at the pieces of death that remained unbudging, unfeeling, threatening to erupt into uncontrollable hemorrhage. It was obvious to Bob and me that complete removal of this widespread cancer was impossible. Reluctantly we began to close the deep, gaping wound.

As we worked we said very little. Extended pain would greet Stanley when the anesthesia wore off. He would feel intense pain, not just that afternoon, but for days and weeks to come.

How would Stanley react to the news of this discovery? Would he be able to accept the fact that his body was harboring a malignant tumor? And, I wondered, will the surgeon be able to accept these results?

Closing the wound took twenty minutes. Still lying face down, Stanley began waking up before the gurney cart arrived. A few minutes passed before he was alert enough to talk. "Dr. Cheatham," he said, his voice slurred with sleep, "were you successful in removing the tumor?"

"Some of it, my friend, but not all." My eyes found his, and a hundred silent conversations passed between us.

The entire surgical team helped wheel the cart carrying Stanley back to his room. As we neared the door, I could see his family waiting. Ann Graber, Marty's wife and a nurse, greeted us. She put her hand on Stanley's shoulder, and with this one touch took responsibility for his post-operative care. Immediately she began to monitor Stanley's vital signs and try to make him more comfortable. He seemed to be completely awake.

Stanley's family looked on in a collective silence that asked, "How is he?"

Bob Wesche and I told them what we knew for sure:

"Stanley has a cancerous tumor.

"It is malignant.

"This means it will not go away.

"We removed what we could. But not all.

"You need to know that Stanley is living with cancer.

"This means that, from now on, each day of life will be a gift."

When Stanley's wife, Annah, and the rest of his family heard these words they showed no emotion. But I could see their eyes blinking back the sadness. Then I glanced into Stanley's eyes. There was no pain, only optimism. "The Lord has brought me through the ordeal of the operation, and He will take care of my needs," he said with great faith.

I have seen numerous patients face the threat of cancer. Some deny it at first. All they can do is hear the news that their lives have an enemy who will not go away. I do not know where Stanley was in all of this. I had already heard so much about his charisma and his character, even though I hadn't asked. In just the few hours I had known this young Kenyan, something had drawn me to him. And that night, as my weary body yielded to sleep and I pulled the sheets up around my head, I asked God to allow Stanley to live.

At nine the next morning, I arrived back at Stanley's hospital room. He was practically sitting up in bed by supporting the weight of his torso with his left elbow. A smile stretched across his face. I saw no hint of pain.

"It is Sunday morning and perhaps you can talk with me," he said. "I want to tell you the story of my early life."

For a moment the thought of cancer disappeared. I moved toward Stanley's bed and sat on a crude wooden stool. Three years earlier I had come to Kenya on safari. Yet the Third World still seemed like a collection of nameless faces. Now, for the first time, I was about to see inside a culture and a country and learn about a man—a Kipsigis tribesman named Stanley Cheborge. And a Christian physician named Mel Cheatham.

TWO

We lived in God's country. My parents had told me so.

In the autumn of 1939 I was six years old. I didn't know what the Garden of Eden looked like, but I had seen Kansas. It stretched for miles outside my bedroom window. Across endless fields I saw hundreds of white-faced cattle littering the horizon. Some of them belonged to my father. He tended them during the day and then worked as a telegrapher at night.

I recall that I heard the words "Great Depression" about as often as my own name. I didn't know what the words meant, but they were mentioned often around the dinner table in the middle of prayers that said we were lucky to have food.

The Great Depression never caught up with me, especially when I could ride with my dad and see the cowboys. They always wore big-brimmed hats, had guns strapped on, and rode horses. I wanted to be like them. No one would hurt me, because cowboys were the good guys and the good guys always lived.

Much too early, however, I learned otherwise. This awful truth became clear to me when my friend, Bobby, died. I remember my father walking into the house. He was a big man, over six feet tall. I always knew when he came in the back door, because the house would shake and everything outside my window would shift, but only for a second.

He came to my bedroom and sat down on the bed next to me. I felt the weight of his body against me and his hand coming to rest on my shoulder.

"Son," he said, "your dad wants to talk to you."

His eyes were serious, and all of a sudden things became very quiet. Then he began to talk. As the words fell out of his mouth, the world that never changed outside my window seemed to shift again.

My father said it was about Bobby. He was one of my friends. We played in the church yard on Sundays after service, sometimes kickball, sometimes tag. And our games were always halted by parents who knew it was a long drive back to our house on the prairie.

"Yesterday," my father said, "Bobby's father went hunting. He had laid his rifle on the dining room table and had gone back outside. Bobby's older brother came in the house and picked up the gun. And then Bobby came in. We don't know how it happened, son, but the gun went off, and Bobby was shot in the head."

"Is he okay, Dad?"

"They raced twenty-five miles to the hospital. They did everything they could, son. But the doctors weren't able to save Bobby's life."

Dad said it was an accident. Bobby's brother didn't mean to do it. And Bobby's father didn't know anyone was in the house at the time. Otherwise he never would have laid his gun on the table.

Until that day in the autumn of 1939, people didn't die. Except when you got old, like grandparents, and uncles, and aunts. But not children.

I can't really remember what Bobby looked like, or even that much about him. I remember my father rubbing his hands across my back, and I can see my breath collect on the bedroom window as the news about Bobby filled my world.

On the day I said good-bye to Bobby, I felt something that I've carried inside ever since. I began asking questions, the kind of questions that over the years have hit me at the speed of light:

Who am I, really?

What am I going to do after I graduate from college?

The demands of work are killing me. How can I stop this crazy pace?

I'm now over fifty years old. What have I done with my life?

Exploring this last question has left me breathless, exhilarated, and at times, weary. It is the reason I wrote this book. In the summer of 1992, years after my world shifted forever that day back in Kansas, I began to re-trace the path that has led me to the most fulfilling and surprising crossroads of life.

There is no pre-planned road map I can give you, no freshly-typed itinerary that explains how I left the still landscape of southeast Kansas, and wound up fifty years later bandaging the wounds and embracing the lives of Kipsigis tribes people at Tenwek Hospital in Kenya, East Africa. But I do know what happened. And I know this story is not mine alone. It belongs to anyone who has ever wondered "Where am I going with my life?" Without meeting Stanley Cheborge and the world he introduced to me, I would never have discovered the answer for myself.

As a schoolboy back in Kansas I had heard of Africa. I had seen the large, color, full-page map of the continent in dog-eared pages of *Life* magazine. There were grotesque masks and wild chieftains wearing wild red plumes that dangled in the face of excited rage. I saw huge elephants that would never be in a zoo. And I imagined a group of khaki-clad Americans, sometimes wearing pith helmets, kneeling next to children in a dim hut.

But Africa looked small compared to my real interest. A classmate of mine in high school had a father who was a doctor. He was a surgeon, and he always seemed very busy. I never got that close to him, even though I'd see him at school plays and sporting events. His black doctor's bag would leave with him whenever the phone rang. He was aloof in a very respectful sort of way.

My family knew my dream of becoming a doctor, because I was not bashful about telling people what I wanted to do when I grew up. That day came sooner than I thought. One afternoon at high school, I was asked to go to the principal's office. There was a phone call from Dr. Grosjean's office. Dr. Grosjean was our family doctor, and I wondered what this was all about.

I walked a little nervously to the school office and a silver-haired secretary handed me the phone.

"Yes, this is Mel Cheatham. . . .

"No, I did not know this was happening to my aunt. . . ."

Would I be available tomorrow? "Tomorrow morning? Yes. Yes, I will be there."

I hung up the phone and could not believe the news. Dr. Grosjean's secretary had told me that my aunt was going in the next day for a radical mastectomy. When the surgeon told my aunt she was going to have a breast removed, she said, "All right. I have a nephew who wants to be a surgeon. I want him to be able to see the operation, so he can know if being a doctor is what he wants to do."

That evening I told my parents about my aunt's wishes, how she had some hesitations, but that in the end, she wanted me to watch the surgery. My parents thought about it and said, yes, I could be excused from my morning classes to watch the operation. This was big. Just the thought of what I was going to do was both indescribable and scary. And that night I never slept.

The next morning, I was greeted at the hospital by the fresh smell of antiseptics. It was nearly summer, and the weather was hot. The hospital had no air conditioning. I started to sweat as I climbed into the white, cotton scrub suit with legs that ran over my feet and onto the floor. A hospital assistant then took me to the operating room, a shining, faded lime green room bathed in bright light. I was so short the scrub nurses stacked a pair of wooden risers on top of each other so I would be high enough to see. Everything was in place — the table, the nurses, the trays of instruments covered by white cloths.

Dr. Harlan J. Brown, the anesthesiologist, was standing at the head of the operating table where my aunt would soon lie. I didn't know what an anesthesiologist was. Next to him, on a machine with several black rubber tubes sprouting out the side, hung a small wooden sign. On it were three words: ANTICIPATE, PLAN, EXECUTE.

"What does that mean?" I asked in a small-sounding voice.

He barked back, "It means anticipate what may come along in life. Plan what you'll do when and if it happens. Then, when the time comes, you'll be able to execute the right response. That's critical in medicine. In medicine, you often don't get the time, the opportunity to respond appropriately, unless you've anticipated and planned."

Three people brought my aunt in on a table with wheels. She was looking up the whole time. Then, they put her to sleep and splashed on red Merthiolate. I was not prepared for what happened next. The surgeon took the scalpel. In one continuous sweep, he made a cut down her chest. A second or two passed before red drops of blood formed. My heart pounded, and all of a sudden I felt very hot.

"Melvin! Melvin!"

I remember looking up and seeing the faces of the nurses staring down at me. As I sat on the cold floor of the hospital hallway, one nurse asked me if I wanted something cool to drink. I had fainted. It took me several minutes to get back on my feet, but soon I was looking through the window into the operating room. In another minute, I found myself next to the doorway. Finally, I was back on my perch.

"Come over here," Dr. Brown said, motioning for me to stand next to him. I looked down at the patient. This was my aunt on the operating table. This was a real person, a person I knew. And the doctors were so matter of fact about what they were doing. It never occurred to me that people would bleed, that they could have their bodies cut into, and altered, then closed up, then wake up later and go on with their lives. I couldn't believe what I was watching. I was both shocked and fascinated.

That afternoon I was back at high school sitting in a classroom. While the teacher asked everyone to picture the Napoleonic Wars, I was too busy reliving my experience from that morning. No one around me knew what I had seen just a few minutes before. When I got home that night I knew I had to go with my parents back to the hospital. I wanted to see that my aunt was put back together and that she was all right. When we got to her room, she was drowsy, but she recognized me.

"How are you, Mel?" she asked in a weak voice. "Did you watch the operation?"

Yes. And then I knew more than ever what I wanted to do in life.

Nineteen fifty-three was not a kind year for college students wanting to get into medical school. Thousands of men had flooded home from the Pacific and Europe after World War II. There were more qualified people applying for far fewer places than I expected. I knew I wanted to go. I made up my mind to go. As a junior in college I had written three medical schools. I had been discouraged at the thought of applying to Harvard Medical School, because so many qualified undergraduates applied—and so few could be accepted. I *had* been accepted by one medical school, Jefferson Medical College in Philadelphia. Even though I planned to enter after only three years of undergraduate schooling completed, I would earn my bachelor's degree in my first year of medical school.

That's what I told the dean of the University of Kansas Medical School, Dr. Clark Wescoe. He was my last interview, part insurance policy, part formality, because I knew where I was headed. From behind his desk he looked right at me and said, "You can go on to the other medical school and earn your bachelor's degree, but if you come to my medical school you won't be considered for admission until you finish your undergraduate work."

Inside I was reeling. "Okay," I said. "That puts me behind the eight ball."

"If you go to medical school before you finish your four years, you'll be putting *yourself* behind the eight ball. You see, Mel, we're not interested in just training medical people. We're interested in building well-rounded individuals, citizens in the community. You can start medical school in the fall. But if you come to my medical school, you'll earn your degree first and you'll be glad you did."

I chewed on those words for days. I was twenty-one years old and confidently unsure of what I was going to do. I was standing at one of life's major intersections. That summer, in my hometown of Winfield, Kansas, the cross streets read Eighth & Millington. Inside the white stucco church building, a robust man with red cheeks was studying in his office. The sign on the glass case near the main door said, "Rev. O. Edgar Wright, Senior

Pastor." To me he was Ed Wright, friend. In a few minutes he would be laying down an unfinished sermon text for the fourth time that day, this time to listen to a young college student tell him how unfair the world was.

He greeted me like I was one of his family. We talked about how school was going, and where I was going. When Ed Wright talked to me, I felt like I was the only person in the world who mattered to him. He made everyone feel that way. In groups, it was something to watch. All the kids in youth group would be playing volleyball at the church. The door from his study would open and Ed would come out. Off would come the suit coat, off would come the tie, and he was right there with us. It was unabandoned joy in action. Ed Wright was a little kid in a big person's body.

For some reason we clicked. I can't count all the dinners I ate with him, Margaret, and their children. One summer Ed invited me to go to California with his family for vacation. Something came up at my house and I never made the trip. But he never stopped investing himself in me and my desire to become a doctor. Ed Wright would never be a physician himself, but he lived out the concern and compassion I knew a good physician needed to have. He took no credit for his "talent" for attending to people's hurts and well-being. He saw his calling to serve others as a gift from God.

It was never more true than that morning we spent together in his office. After a few minutes my concerns about my future were all out, and he asked the question that froze me to my chair: "What do *you* want to do, Mel?"

"I don't want to wait. I want to go to medical school this fall," I said. "Then I meet a dean who tells me I need to finish my fourth year. But if I do that, I forfeit a sure bet—my acceptance at another school."

"And what do think you would gain by forfeiting the chance to complete your fourth year and learn things you won't find in medical school?"

Ed Wright had done it again. He had put the question, the choice, in my lap. It was as if he were saying, "Mel, I have total confidence in you. I believe in you. You are a mature young man, who can decide for himself. Just remember, you're not making a decision that affects the next year, but one that will affect the rest of your life."

"What is the real 'sure bet'? Is it going on to medical school now, or investing the next year in studies that may eventually help you better understand your patients? Think about the courses Dr. Wescoe wants you to take. Psychology will help you know how your patients think. Religion will give you insights into how people approach God. History will help you understand the world at large, a world you may shape in some small yet very real way someday."

I left Ed Wright's office that afternoon, took a right turn out the door and never looked back at Jefferson Medical College.

That fall I began my fourth year of undergraduate work. I exchanged my seat in Human Anatomy at medical school for classes in religion and the humanities. The following year I reapplied to the University of Kansas Medical School and was accepted. At the time I couldn't fully appreciate the impact of this decision, except that it kept me in Kansas, where my world grew larger and less simple.

In the fall of my first year of medical school I found myself sitting in cavernous lecture halls, operating on cadavers, and coming face to face with more of the human body than I could possibly memorize for one final exam. Every day was a new lesson in Mortality. Lecture. Listen. Study. Test. Then repeat the entire cycle again until you thought you had it. The skeletal system. The nervous system. The brain. It demanded every bit of concentration, every drop of desire I had, because someday I knew my textbook descriptions would be living, breathing people placed in my care. Someday came too soon.

That next fall, I got a phone call from my parents. Ed Wright had suffered a stroke. He was only forty-five and now partially paralyzed on the right side. The report also showed kidney failure. I was not yet a doctor, and never quite a son, but with Ed it didn't matter. At the earliest possible break in my schedule, I drove home so I could be with him.

When I arrived at his bedside, my landscape had changed again. And I knew Ed Wright would never be the same. The energetic man who had once dived for stray volleyballs lay on his back with one arm and leg nearly paralyzed. As the months crawled by, Ed's condition worsened. And there was nothing I could do.

Two years later I found myself standing next to his hospital bed. I was now a senior in medical school. He was still a relatively young man, but his health was rapidly deteriorating. I looked on anxiously as a nurse failed to find a vein in his arm for the IV tube that would help keep him alive. Nothing worked. Finally, I took the needle, and after several misses found the vein. It was the second hardest moment for me to bear throughout the whole ordeal. In a few minutes a team of aides walked in briskly and wheeled Ed through a pair of swinging doors and into the X-ray department. It was the last time I saw him alive.

That Sunday morning, I came into the church service and learned that Ed had died. I wasted no time in driving to the hospital. There I found Margaret with her children. As I hugged her, she was gracious. And in her loss, she was smiling. She knew Ed didn't need those IV tubes now, because now he was at home with his Maker.

"Before Ed died," she said to me, "he requested an autopsy and there was only one person he wanted to assist Dr. Grosjean.

And that was you. He wanted it this way, because he wanted you to have this learning experience." It was Ed's final act of giving to me. Even after he was done breathing in this life, Ed Wright still wanted to help Mel Cheatham.

The autopsy was an overwhelming experience. In those few hours with Dr. Grosjean, who had operated on my aunt, I stood over the man who had guided me into medicine. And I became ever more aware of the preciousness of life. As a physician, I knew the time would come when I would have to say goodbye to other friends, and I have. But no one has left me at such a loss as Ed.

"What would you like to do, Mel?"

I heard Ed Wright asking me that question continually for the next several years. There were big decisions to be made. And the breakneck pace of medical school didn't slow up.

I decided to follow my instinct—to pursue my strongest interest and greatest challenge—and go into neurosurgery. It was a very young field. In the late 1950s, little was known about what causes tumors of the brain and spinal cord, much less how to cure them. There were no early-detection devices and no way to peer through a patient's skull and identify a tumor growing out of control, threatening to overwhelm the body.

Surgery could remove a tumor, but not if the intruder was malignant. Too often that discovery fell to the neurosurgeon. Success relied on skilled hands and precise judgment. Practicing those three words on Dr. Harlan J. Brown's sign were no longer an option. I now had to live and breathe the words "Anticipate, Plan, and Execute," if my patients and my career were to survive.

Eleven months away from graduation, my eyes began drifting away from this goal. I did not regret the distraction. I met a young English woman named Sylvia. Based in Kansas City, she worked as a hostess for TWA. She told me her dream was to work for British Airways and fly from London, where she had grown up, to Hong Kong. Her accent and her charm stayed with me after our first date. At first, finding time to be in love during medical school had seemed impossible. Now finding the time was inescapable. In October we became engaged. Seven months later, the day before I graduated from the University of Kansas Medical School, we were married.

The years that followed were busy with preparation for a life of medicine. An internship at the University of California, San Francisco. A year of general surgery residency at the University of Kansas. Two years with a general surgical assignment as a surgeon for the 328th Fighter Wing at Richards-Gebaur Air Force Base. Then a four-year residency in neurosurgery at the University of Kansas. And finally a graduate degree in neuroanatomy while a post-doctorate fellow for the National Institutes of Health.

Eight years went by, and Sylvia and I decided we wanted to raise our family in the Midwest. We wanted a town that slept through the night and didn't wake to the ceaseless noise of the city. We found our wish no less than 1,900 miles to the left of Kansas City, in Ventura, California. This town, an hour northwest of Los Angeles, hugged the Pacific Ocean shore. And we embraced its pace from day one.

Ventura was where the road ended and my practice began. Starting out, I found myself one of only three neurosurgeons in the entire county. No single hospital was fully equipped to handle neurosurgery, so my partners and I drove the freeways and county roads, carrying our own surgical instruments to the next operation. Life in the fast lane became more of a reality each passing day.

A doctor's schedule is unforgiving. Beepers and pagers had not yet been heard of. Instead the telephone ran my life. There was always one more request to come to the hospital, one more patient who needed help. "Now, doctor, we need you now!" I drove my own shuttle service from home, to office, to surgery, back to the office, then back home as night blurred into morning. Somewhere, in between calls, the surgical schedules, and the weeks on call, our family grew. First a son, Michael, then a daughter, Elizabeth, and another son, Robert. By 1983, seventeen years after Ventura became our home, my neurosurgical practice had grown into an eighty- to ninety-hour-week commitment without limits. I needed to call a time out.

The decision was made one weekend when Sylvia and I were in Los Angeles. We were standing in the lobby of a travel agency surrounded by huge, full-color banners of Hawaiian beaches and London's Big Ben. Without warning, a travel agent dressed in a dark blue blazer shot a question at us from behind a row of file cabinets.

"Why don't you go on a photographic safari to Africa?"

I looked at the wall and saw a family of zebra grazing across a huge, glossy colored savannah. Under their noses were the large, orange letters, KENYA.

"Why not try a trip to Kenya to see the animals? You will love it."

The round-faced man we'd known less than four minutes moved out from behind the counter, and while his words were still fresh, he handed me a couple of brochures.

"No, I don't think so," I said politely.

Translation: I'm too pressured to say "Yes, we'll go." But if you give my family and me time to think about it over the next few days, we'll probably buy the entire package and go on a 20,000-mile, round-trip adventure we never thought about before.

Which is exactly what happened. Now, I would be part of that American family I had seen as a child kneeling in a mud hut. I would visit Africa, but I wouldn't stay there. I only had enough interest and film to last me two weeks. After all, this was only a safari.

Six weeks later, our Boeing 747 touched down in Nairobi. Straggling into the open-air terminal after enduring twenty hours, 10,000 miles and ten time zones, we met our human guide to Africa. He was a uniformed Kenyan guide from Rhino Safaris. He looked at me, extended his open palm and said, "You can call me Moses, because that is my name." Those were the most words I would hear him speak at one time for the next fourteen days.

Moses led our family out of the Jomo Kenyatta International Airport and into the vibrating core of downtown Nairobi. The noise could have passed for Los Angeles. As our van came to rest on a curb in front of a bustling hotel, angry car horns and seas of foot traffic evaporated behind a revolving door. Once on the twelfth floor of the hotel, I peeled back the curtains and saw a city crawling below as the air conditioner cooled my sweaty face. Later, as I walked outside, I discovered the Africa I had seen in *Life* magazine as a youngster had never looked like this. The caravan of downtown traffic exhausted my lungs with the smell of diesel fumes. One-legged beggars huddled on corners with cardboard signs pleading for small change. Big fluorescent signs announced "Barclays Bank," "British Airways," "Peugeot." This was Africa in the twilight of the twentieth century. It was over-populated and under-paved with more shop-keepers and stray children than the city or the mind could take in.

We did the Safari. Or you could say the Safari did us. It began when Moses ushered us into a combi-van, a diesel-coughing, metal-paneled box that accelerated our exodus from the city into an uncharted network of dirt roads. As I looked out my window I saw the landscape change from gray masonry block buildings and men on motor scooters, to mud huts bordered by naked, waving children.

The parade of barefoot women going to market gave way to abandoned savannahs. The roar of the diesel engine was our only company, the only disruption in a nearly silent world inhabited only by the wind's whisper. We were amazed to see young boys tending cattle so far from any other signs of civilization. It was the beginning of an 1,800-mile journey that took us to the foot of Mt. Kenya, to the plains of Samburu where we witnessed our first "kill." At first, the thought of one animal devouring another seemed offensive. Yet, in their natural habitat, seeing one creature kill another as a source of food made me realize we were witnessing a created order filled with unforgiving awe.

We were captivated by the animals and the great expanse they roamed. On the shores of Lake Nakuru, one entire end of the lake appeared pink. As we rolled closer in the van, we realized the pink was actually thousands of flamingos standing in the shallow water.

"Look at that," became a phrase of wonder and delight as we spied lions, impala, and wildebeest through the binoculars. I remember seeing giraffe, lean, towering, and stiff-necked. The van slowed, and their heads turned. The horizon that had bounced wildly for the past half-hour now became frozen still under a hot sun.

"Look how still they are," someone said, in a hushed voice. In this land where we were guests, our words took on a reverence for the animals who were here long before we were. I had seen their brown and orange blotched skins in city zoos, but I had never appreciated how they survived at home, these strange creatures who walked with stilts and moved with the gentlest of steps. Moses crept closer with the van. I could see that only their mouths moved, as the giraffe munched on tree leaves. I raised my camera and saw the long, animated lips working for food. A picture might capture a split-second of life. But the bigger photograph was developing inside me. Its breadth and expanse knew no borders.

Our van crawled past giraffe toward green fields sprinkled with brush. Along the way, we found other permanent residents. In the wide-open fields, where shallow pools of water remained after heavy rains, we saw zebra. They looked totally calm, undaunted by how their Creator had made their striped hides so entertaining and bold. As we rolled past, our attention and our cameras became focused in the same breath. The zebra didn't pay us one blink of attention as they drank from a common pool.

This was a prelude to other sights that waited minutes away. Although time seemed to stop as we marveled at these creatures, we were still racing against the sun. In a little bit, we would miss the animals when they retreated into the bush, said Moses. Then he shifted the van to a new level of speed and chaos. Ruts suddenly turned into small ski jumps as the vehicle catapulted through the slow-baking heat. I had ridden roller coasters that were smoother and seemed safer. We were in a race against nature. The finish line lay waiting over a small crest. Moses brought us to a stop. Collectively, the entire Cheatham family rose from our seats.

"Off to your left," said Moses. No other words were required. Not more than a few yards from our front bumper stood elephants. Their huge ears flinched, their trunks reached into a shallow pool. There must have been fifteen or twenty of them, all perfectly content to let us drive by. We had caught them taking a bath. I was struck, however, that we were the ones who had really been captured by the weight of their stature.

As tourists, our curiosity had held us captive to this unclammored corner of the world. The combi-van would stop.

Cameras would click. And after an all too brief look at these creatures, the scene would rock and shift again as the vehicle lurched ahead, careening our curious party deeper down the trail.

"Dad, look! Vultures!" Robert spotted several wide-wing-spanned birds circling overhead. Without fanfare they descended on the carcass of what had been a wildebeest or a gazelle. Nature, again, was oblivious to our presence. In a matter of days, after the vultures were done, the hot, equatorial sun would bleach the animal's bones. Such is life and death on the African plains.

While the sun burned overhead in Kenya, it was night time in Ventura. In my mind's eye I could see one of my partners at the hospital poring over a patient's chart, handling the critical decisions that would help keep another person alive. What would I tell them about this land, and the new signs of life that began emerging on the horizon as our combi rolled up the path? It was a collection of huts looming larger. The vehicle pulled up, and out of the dust emerged a sprinkling of men and women and children. These were Maasai tribes people, Moses told us. They were tall and slender and they didn't stop staring.

From my reading and Moses' description, I knew I was seeing the people of a thousand-year-old culture, dressed in bright red native dress. I noticed a woman walking across the plains bringing water to a thirsty family. On her head elegantly rode a ten gallon container. It needed no balancing of the hand. Hours behind her lay a distant stream or pool now a little less full. Back home, a boy, clothed in only a suka sheet and armed with a spear, guarded his cattle.

My itinerary had not prepared me for encounters like this. As our combi-van idled, my mind and heart engaged the path of the Maasai woman.

Your families live miles apart.

How do you deal with sickness, animal attacks, disease?
What happens if your appendix ruptures?
What do you do if you start bleeding and there's no way to stop it?
Where do you go when your bush medicine, the herbs and other plants and mysterious elixirs you believe in, fail?

I looked at these Maasai villagers and saw hundreds of health questions staring back at me from silent black eyes. I had to give them the benefit of history. Obviously they had survived for generations, but at what cost and at what pain could that have been avoided?

Their health needs, whether they realized them or not, disturbed me. Our combi-van stopped at the entrance of one of the Maasai villages. As the chief of this particular village waited, we decided to pay $40 to get a first-hand view of African tribal life.

We were led through an opening in the six-foot-tall barrier of thicket and bramble which surrounded the village and kept cattle safely inside, away from hungry lions. This tourist ritual led to a clearing of dry dirt and cow dung. With each step a cloud of dust formed. There were pairs of small children, many of whom had coughs and runny noses. Their faces, like the adults, were covered with flies. They stood outside huts plastered with mud and more cow dung. The roofs were covered with sticks, mud, and grass. There were no windows, only a low doorway through which we could bow down to reach the smoky darkness inside.

This is where the Maasai lived, on a dirt floor, beside a fire that filled the hut with smoke, and offered cooking by day and warmth by night. Once outside the hut, I covered my eyes from the sun that now seemed seven times brighter than before we had gone in.

In four minutes I had seen more of Africa than had rushed past me in hundreds of safari miles. And yet my Africa remained silent, locked away in a language I couldn't understand. In the few minutes of peering at their homes and their way of life, we exchanged not one word. Moses may have brought us out of Nairobi, but without a common language, I remained a prisoner, free to speak but not to be understood.

We were escorted, briskly, through the village. And as we made our hasty exit, passing Maasai women wearing intricate beaded necklaces, armbands, and bracelets, our cultural tour became an impromptu sale of panga knives, spears, and clubs.

Through the flash of merchandise as Maasai men beckoned us to buy, I saw the children, lined up and standing barefoot in the dirt. I wondered what diseases were roaming through them. How many years would it be until they would fall victim to malaria, tuberculosis, hepatitis, intestinal parasites, and other diseases?

I stepped back into the combi-van and turned around to see the Maasai villagers. The chief stood by the entrance way, his spear firmly planted in the ground. A few children decided to wave. I stuck my arm through the open window and waved back.

These were faces that had no names. They were human beings I would never really know. A feeling of sadness swept over me. In the summer of 1983 I had reached Africa and shaken hands with a country I was unable to converse with, much less comprehend.

What would you like to do, Mel?

I wanted to put a name to the million faces I met. I wanted to know the real Africa.

That day, on the road heading northwest from Nairobi, he was not that far away—the person who would introduce me to a new world, his world, which was soon to become my own.

THREE

It was one of those little-known facts that caught my eye and wouldn't let go:

There are two major geographic formations on the African Continent recognizable to space shuttle pilots orbiting miles above: the Nile River, and the Great Rift Valley.

I laid the magazine in my lap and looked out the window. Through the double-paned safety glass of the 747, I could see one wide, continuous, rumpled blanket of earth. From 36,000 feet, the Great Rift Valley in western Kenya extended in all directions. There were no scattered buildings, no roadways, no signatures of contemporary Western civilization. I saw only miles of brown earth interrupted now and then by a thin sheet of clouds. While I looked over the plane's wing to the parched earth below, a voice crackled through the speaker overhead.

"Out your window you see the Great Rift Valley that stretches for more than 5,400 miles. It is a crack in the African plate that, in length, exceeds one quarter of the earth's circumference."

I realized this was probably my last look at Africa. I had spent three weeks bouncing along safari trails. I had captured dozens of wild animals with my telephoto lens. Along the way I had focused on a million random images from wandering children to countless women carrying firewood on their backs to the endless parade of humanity that collected in Nairobi.

To me, they all belonged to the tribe of Strangers. In the noise of native tongues I couldn't understand, I would catch a glance from a child. In an instant we would communicate and understand how little each of us knew about the other. It was a mutually curious look through which both of us said, "You are someone I've seen and read about in books. You smile back at me, but I do not understand what you are saying. We can shake hands, and for a second our worlds will touch. But I will never know your name. And you will never really know my home."

After an overland safari, driven by the hope of seeing big game, what I knew of the Kenyan people could fill a thimble. I looked out the plane's window and imagined a Kenya I had never met, a tribe scattered on the desert floor, an ancient culture stirring on the edge of dawn.

They might be from the Kikuyu tribe, the Meru tribe, or the Kipsigis, a group living near the equator in western Kenya. My mind flew to Ventura, returned to the Great Rift Valley, and traveled back again. One moment I was operating at Community Memorial Hospital looking down at a patient, preparing to make the first incision. The next moment I was looking down over the wing of the plane on a culture I didn't know.

I imagined a young Kipsigis asleep inside a cool, dark hut. He lay curled upon a hard dirt floor no bigger than our kitchen floor in Ventura, with seven or eight other relatives of various ages. I imagined him wrapped in the smoke of the family's cooking fire that was never allowed to die.

The young man would be getting up soon. He would step over his kin and walk to the opening in the hut, invaded with bright sunlight. He was not the first one up. When the young

Kipsigis walked across the patted earth outside the hut, chickens would scatter. He could see his family's goats sprinkled on the land, and he knew he would soon join them in the fields as they grazed. What would his day hold? How many miles would he walk before I was out of Africa? How would he continue to survive the daily threats of wild animals and unfriendly neighboring tribes? I rode with these questions all the way to London. Three days and eight time zones later, our jet taxied across the runway at Los Angeles International Airport. Soon, we were in the car, crawling up Route 101 in the late-afternoon rush hour to our home in Ventura.

I wondered where the Kipsigis boy and his goats were by now. At the moment, my world probably moved slower than his, as we sat looking out the window at thousands of nameless strangers from our tribe, all inching forward on the freeway. When we finally pulled up in the driveway, I spoke the ancient word that signaled a journey's end: "Shower." Then I took one with much glee. And slept for thirteen hours straight.

Community Memorial Hospital was waiting for my return. The next morning I walked down the shiny, waxed hallways that took me to the surgical floor nursing station. They were slightly brighter than the dirt floor of the Maasai Chief's home that had been tamped and smoothed by bare feet.

Through the slalom course of nurses, visitors, and equipment carts, one of my surgeon friends spotted me and called out.

"Dr. Livingstone, I presume?"

"Good morning, Dan," I said, as we shook hands. I could tell he wasn't ready to let go.

"How many times did your beeper go off in the middle of Kenya?"

"None," I replied. "The hospital answering service couldn't find the area code for Rhino Safaris. So I had all the calls forwarded to you."

We stood in the busy hallway and I realized that within a few minutes, I would be in my office across the street seeing the first of about twenty patients that day. The only pressure facing my friend, now off call, was how to get to the golf course in time to tee off.

"Now Mel, before we part company, tell me, in twenty-five words or less, what Kenya was like."

"Do you have a month?"

"Let me check my calendar." Dan smiled, grabbed an armful of patient charts, and disappeared into one of the rooms. My vacation trip was over. It was time to go to work. In neurosurgery, life barely stops to breathe. For a family, cradling the future of a loved-one with a brain tumor, nothing else matters than what you can do for them right then. On that first morning back in the office, "right now" wouldn't wait even for a first cup of coffee.

My first week back in the office started out full-throttle. It was like every other week—filled with so many responsibilities, and so little time. Morning rounds on patients started at 7:00 a.m. Nearly every day I would be in the operating room for as many as three neurosurgical procedures. Frequently I'd assist my associates with their operations, usually one or two evenings a week. Then, at the office, I had to make time to see follow-up patients and new patients who were referred for consultation and possible surgery.

Weekends brought little rest in the morning, when I was back at the hospital checking on patients. Then I would catch up on dictating reports, hospital records, and consultations. Sandwiched somewhere in all of these commitments were hospital staff and committee meetings. Always there seemed to be a stack of messages waiting. Always, always I was behind schedule, or late, because patients, families, and emergencies took more time. Just when I felt I was catching up, I faced the necessity of finding time to read and study in order to stay current with new advances in medicine and neurosurgery. On top of my practice, I found myself serving as President of the California Association of Neurological Surgeons–the California State Neurosurgical Society–that represented the 510 neurosurgeons in the state.

Every third or fourth week, my "typical" fourteen-hour day went into overdrive as I went on call. This meant that for twenty-four hours-a-day I was responsible not only for my own patients, but for those of my three partners as well. Any emergency neurosurgery that needed to be performed during that time was left to me.

The calls could come at any time–in the middle of the night or while I was brushing my teeth. Often the phone would ring within three minutes of our sitting down to dinner. And when it did, the only thing that mattered was knowing how to keep a patient alive another day, so he or she could regain health and live for months and, hopefully, years.

I did not thrive on being pulled out of bed at 4:00 a.m. by a ringing telephone. Sometimes, at the end of a week of being on call, with my body crying for sleep and my nerve endings starting to fray, I would rather have heard the sound of a dentist's drill than the high-pitched cry of a pager going off. However, I never tired of the challenge of doing everything in my power to be a good doctor to my patients. If anything, I did not know when to quit. In fact, there were times I poured every drop of energy into a lengthy surgery or weeks of post-operative care, until my own health began to suffer. How do you quit paying attention to a forty-two-year-old father with a brain tumor, who may not live unless you make the extra phone call or the four, five, six trips to the hospital to determine what he needs to stay alive? At what point do you say to yourself, "I've done enough?" When do you admit you cannot remain alert another minute without something so simple as a good night's sleep?

I would fight with these questions as I drove from home to the hospital and back again. Often, in the most congested reality of California life, the paved savannah of freeway traffic, I found my greatest sanctuary. After coming home from Africa, I realized something in my world had changed. The people in my home town didn't look the same. Rushing through the crosswalks, the mothers looked more harried. The drivers I could see in my rear-view mirror looked more bored. I would get behind a truck filled with Arrowhead Drinking Water, obviously bound for another family who couldn't swallow what the city's reservoirs had to give them, and I would think of the Maasai woman I had met. I knew that on the other side of the world, she was walking several hours in one direction to fill her two-gallon container with water, then walk back on the same beaten path, all for the sake of her thirsty family.

The Arrowhead truck would turn off, but my thoughts stayed with the Maasai woman. I would pull up to our driveway, flick on the automatic garage door opener, park the car and go inside. Sylvia would be in the kitchen fixing dinner. A few weeks after returning from Kenya, we were just sitting down when Sylvia said, "I noticed by the phone today, a newsletter from Project Hope. I wonder if they need any more doctors to work for two months in Jamaica."

I wondered too. Jamaica had a special attraction for the Cheathams, though not for the same reason shared by thousands of vacation-starved Americans. Years earlier, we had signed up to serve for a month on the hospital ship "Hope" anchored in Kingston.

This was not a chapter of life I wanted to re-open. Jamaica had been a dream for me, one of those "what if" opportunities I thought would never come around again. And I had no one to blame but Dr. William P. Williamson, a professor of neurosurgery at the University of Kansas Medical School, who walked into my life one day while I was still scratching the surface of medicine as a freshman. The brain stores certain moments in its vault, and the day I met Dr. Williamson is safe in my permanent collection. It happened one morning when our instructor, Dr. Paul G. Roof, chairman of the anatomy department, arranged for our class to go to the medical center for clinical training. Once we were seated in the lecture hall, he walked in. He was the most immaculately-dressed man I had ever seen, the kind of figure that quiets a room of all talking.

With a proud smile, Dr. Roof addressed the stranger standing next to him in front of the room and said, "Dr. Williamson, I've found this class very accomplished in neuro-anatomy. I think you'll find them well prepared for your lecture."

With that, Dr. Roof sat down, and for the next sixty minutes, this impeccable presenter proceeded to demonstrate to 110 self-assured, first-year medical students how little we really knew about the field of neurosurgery. It was a fact he made painfully obvious, revealing our lack of knowledge with genuine respect. And he did so with utter brilliance. I was struck with this man of towering intellectual ability who seemed more interested in what I could learn rather than what he knew. That morning, the field of medicine narrowed drastically for me. Because of Dr. Williamson I decided to go into neurosurgery.

After graduating from medical school, I didn't see Dr. Williamson until a year later when I returned to the University of Kansas as a general surgery resident. Three years after that I was standing next to him as a neurosurgical resident. This was where I belonged, in neurosurgery, working alongside the guest lecturer in medical school who showed me how much I still needed to know. Except something had changed about him.

He operated with the same precision and confidence displayed in that first morning lecture. But he was not the same

Dr. Williamson I had known before. I knew he had just come back to Kansas from spending two months on the ship *Hope* off the coast of Peru, South America. For sixty straight days he had treated sick, malnourished nationals who found their way onto this floating medical outpost docked off shore. For sixty days without let-up he held babies who were so thin he could barely find veins in their arms big enough for a needle that would give them fluids or blood while he operated on their brains or spines. This challenge paled against a greater backdrop of desperation. Dr. Williamson told me how researchers had flown in cages of guinea pigs to conduct experiments that would further medical work designed to help prevent life-threatening diseases. The research never took place because a group of Peruvians were so hungry they ate the guinea pigs.

"These people don't need a brain surgeon like me," he said. "They need soap to keep clean. They need to learn about modern sanitation. They need baby shots. They need basic health care if they're to live." This articulate man who could explain intricate surgical procedures with the ease of reciting his street address became tongue tied as he tried to describe the plight of people who were living on the edge of despair.

I carried Dr. Williamson's vision with me out to Ventura. Now, I was the brain surgeon who wanted to take my medicine to a nation in need. I started pursuing organizations who could use my skills, who could send me somewhere, anywhere where there were people in need of a doctor.

For months, I called and wrote missions agencies and humanitarian service organizations. In between caring for three small children, Sylvia typed applications and read response letters that seemed to have been written by the same person, "We regret to inform you that . . ." No one had any specific demand for a neurosurgeon. They had every need for a doctor who could perform the simple, everyday operations that didn't require a scalpel: shots, physicals, delivering babies, teaching basic hygiene, everything my friend and mentor Dr. Williamson had seen and touched and lived.

In 1970, the year after I became a board-certified neurosurgeon, I learned that the ship *Hope* was sailing to Kingston, Jamaica. In a corner of the Project Hope newsletter, was a classified ad that whispered:

> The Ship *Hope* announces the need for a neurosurgeon to
> serve on board for a two-month stay in Kingston, Jamaica.
> Contact Dr. William B. Walsh.

The word "neurosurgeon" jumped off the page. There were questions, though. How would we travel with a one-year-old son? Since families were not allowed to live on board, how would Sylvia care for him, our seven-year-old Elizabeth, and eight-year-old Michael? How would they remain, alone, in a village on shore for eight weeks?

For a neurosurgeon, two months is forever. It was the equivalent of putting my partners on call for sixty days. Having just opened a practice in Ventura, such a leave would be crippling. And impossible.

I dialed Jamaica and said I could come for one month, but not two. Their response was no. With a medical license as our passport, the desire to travel as a family to another country didn't fade. It grew. In 1982 when the Afghan war broke out, in the blitz of mail that landed daily in my office, I spotted a notice buried in the back of a professional journal:

> Lady Reading Hospital in Peshawar, Pakistan is seeking a
> neurosurgeon to treat Afghan refugees traveling over the
> Khyber Pass. All interested individuals should contact . . .

My curiosity was stirred again. The next morning before breakfast, I dialed the thirteen-digit number, so that the telephone rang at 6:00 p.m. in the city of Peshawar. There was no answer. The next morning I tried again. Again, the same tired dial tone rang in my ear. I called back in ten minutes, only to get a busy signal. This happened thirty-five times for the next month. I never spoke to the Lady Reading Hospital, and I never learned if they found the neurosurgeon they wanted.

Peru. Kingston. Pakistan. Ventura. In my mind I took a global tour and came back home to our dining room table where Sylvia and I sat. I came home to the realization that God must put people in particular places for reasons no one can explain. He had put me on the coast of Southern California where my life had come to rest in Ventura. I could work the rest of my career, never leave the country, and accept my place.

Except I had left. I had gone to Africa and now I was different. Now, my world was larger than strip malls and crowded exit ramps. Now it included permanent images of Maasai children too tired to brush the flies off their foreheads and questions about their health too complicated to answer.

"These people don't need a brain surgeon, Mel. They need soap, and baby shots, and the basic health essentials to stay alive."

What was I going to do with these words?

Have you ever had a question nibble on your conscience? Have you ever rolled over in the middle of the night and felt so confronted with who you are and where your life is going that you can't sleep? I tried to picture myself in a village handing out bars of soap to children. I wondered if a vaccine shot and a lecture on public health would make a difference.

These thoughts rumbled inside me when I went to bed and one Saturday morning just after I woke up. I was propped up in bed, reading the *Los Angeles Times*. A cup of coffee sat on the nightstand. The television was on, and I was ready to practice my ritual. The kids called it "channel surfing." You let your thumb ride over the remote control buttons, skipping channels until you caught something of interest. Suddenly I saw a man on the screen who looked familiar. He seemed like his dad, but only younger. I turned the volume up. He even sounded a little like his dad, too. "I just returned from Calcutta, India, where people live in one of the most crowded, poverty stricken corners of the world," the man said to the talk show host. "Can you imagine living in a cardboard house on the sidewalk, surrounded by thousands of people within one-square mile?"

No, I can't, I thought, as I nursed my coffee.

I heard Sylvia walk into the bedroom. "Come take a look and tell me who this man is," I said to her. But before she could guess, the talk show host told her.

"People must ask you: Haven't you, Franklin Graham, ever desired to preach like your father?"

"My father has been called by God to preach the Gospel of Jesus Christ. He's been called to preach in the great stadiums of the world. God has called me to the gutters—to minister to the lowly, the poor, the downtrodden in our world. They're the people who have little or no material possessions, who are without food and clothing and, often, without Christ. That's what our ministry, Samaritan's Purse, is all about."

This young man, with his well-defined chin, intense eyes, and rolling voice, looked and sounded so much like his father, Billy Graham. I had seen Billy for years on television, hearing him give the simple, profound message of the Christian faith, a message I had believed for myself as a child.

I wondered if Sylvia knew what I was thinking. "Remember when I first began wishing I'd had the chance to work with Billy Graham?" I asked.

"Yes," she replied. "Are you still wishing?"

I turned back to the television and saw what looked like a crude hospital and a young doctor wearing a stethoscope leaning over a frail, elderly African man.

"That's what physicians do through World Medical Mission," Franklin said. "We say, 'Here's a community of people who need help. They need medical attention, surgery, casts for broken limbs, ways to prevent tuberculosis, malaria, and other diseases. We will connect you with a hospital where you can offer your medical skills for a month. You pay your own expenses to get there; we'll make sure you have a place to live.' And we're not looking for doctors and their families who will come for a vacation. We want them to work."

As Graham's voice trailed off, the faces of children dissolved into a shot of the talk show host who was still gripped by the scenes he'd just seen. He sat back in his chair and said, "Now Franklin, tell me, you actually have physicians, nurses, and other medical personnel contact you and take time off, take a month or more from their jobs, just to volunteer with World Medical Mission somewhere in the world?"

"Yes, sir, we do."

"We're going to put the World Medical Mission address and phone number on the screen. . . ."

Without taking my eyes off the television, I reached over to the bedside table and picked up a pen and paper. Then I wrote as fast as I could. I looked over at Sylvia. She was writing, too. "Do you think Franklin Graham has been reading our mail for the last several years?" I wondered aloud.

"When are you going to write your letter?" she asked.

"About as soon as I can turn on the computer." I realized I didn't need a brain surgeon to tell me what was going on in my head. The questions I wanted to ask Franklin Graham flooded my mind.

Where overseas are you sending physicians to work?

Is it true what you said about going for four weeks?

Would you consider a family of five from Ventura, California?

Would you take a neurosurgeon, even if he hasn't performed general surgery in the past twenty-two years?

I typed out these questions as fast as I could think. Yet, there were other questions I wasn't quite ready to consider. Questions like, "What is a fifty-two-year-old neurosurgeon doing leaving his practice for four or more weeks at a time?" And "Why would I stuff my life in a set of Samsonite luggage and give a small chapter of it to people I will probably never see again? Why Mel Cheatham? And why now?"

I had two possible answers. The first one had been given to me by Dean Clark Wescoe. He once said, "Mel, every man ought to have two careers. And he should start the second by the time he's fifty." He should have known. This was a man who became a full college professor at twenty-six, dean of the medical school at twenty-nine, and chancellor of the university by the time he was thirty-six.

I was past fifty and something was happening to me inside. Just the weeks before, it seemed, I had watched my children crawling around on the floor and learning to walk. Now they were grown up and leaving messages on the phone machine about when they'd be coming home from college. I checked my appointment calendar to see what year it was. It seemed like yesterday I was holding my diploma from medical school with flash bulbs exploding all around me. Since that day I had lived a lifetime. A minute ago, my blind date, a young woman named Sylvia, was telling me how she went to work for Trans World Airlines. Now, my wife of twenty-six years was willing to go with me overseas, not to sightsee, but to work. I had come to believe Dean Wescoe's theory. I just had never believed I would reach fifty.

I had a second reason for considering serving overseas: just because I wanted to. It had nothing to do with being bored with my practice or wrestling with a midlife crisis. It had everything to do with trusting what would happen if Franklin

Graham ever read my letter and said, "There's a place that needs you."

I had no doubt about Sylvia's commitment to the trip. From working with Becky Williams at World Medical Mission to secure airplane reservations to making sure each family member had exactly what he or she needed for the trip, Sylvia was the consumate organizer. When we first met, she always dressed very properly. An "English Lady" who had grown up in London, she had always worn a hat on Sunday, and invariably donned white gloves. Now, as a veteran of family trips to Europe, she would channel her dignity, compassion, and efficiency by handling all the details an overseas trip demanded.

Several months after I mailed my letter to World Medical Mission, we received an invitation to work at Presbyterian Medical Center in Chonju, South Korea. When Sylvia heard the news, she had only one apprehension. "I can go just about anywhere in the world, as long as I don't have to wring a chicken's neck."

Her wish was granted in Chonju, a city of over 800,000 people. For five weeks I worked with the hospital's medical staff, helping perform surgeries on patients who had come from miles away. Many had walked. Had I not seen Franklin Graham on television that morning, had I not hurriedly typed a letter and mailed it to World Medical Mission, had I not gone to South Korea I never would have met people whose suffering and sacrifices taught me what it means to serve others.

While there I heard an almost unbelievable story of faith that involved Dr. David Seel, a brilliant surgeon and Christian missionary. It was about a Korean hospital guard who had been called out of a prayer service. Just as he was explaining how much he trusted Jesus Christ, the man was told that his seven-year-old son had been hit by a truck and killed.

This slender Korean wept. In the midst of his incredible grief, he continued to believe God loved him. Eventually, as retribution, the trucking company awarded the man a generous financial payment and he gave every dollar to build a new church in his son's name. When construction slowed, due to lack of funds, the man learned that wealthy people will sometimes pay for a person's eyes to be used as transplant organs. Then the Korean man asked his friend, Dr. David Seel, if *he* could sell one of his own eyes so the church could be finished. Dr. Seel said no and explained why.

When this story was told in Korea some months later, a wealthy businessman heard it. He didn't believe even a wisp of Christianity, but was so moved he donated the money needed to finish the church. In the process the businessman decided to give his life to Jesus Christ.

In South Korea I learned God can bring good out of the greatest tragedies. And I learned something else: The decision to serve was not mine alone. Rather it was a choice our family made. So I shouldn't have been surprised to see my oldest son, Michael, a pre-med college student at Stanford University, eagerly wanting to help me in surgery. I shouldn't have been concerned when Sylvia was asked to teach an English-as-a-second-language class to Korean women; she pulled it off with little preparation. I shouldn't have been surprised that daughter Elizabeth used her writing talents to produce a new set of public relations materials the hospital needed. And I shouldn't have been surprised to learn that, while I was spending hours each day in the operating room, our seventeen-year-old son Robert was teaching English to nurses and physicians, as well as leading a Bible study for Korean junior high school students.

South Korea confirmed there was indeed a place for a doctor on the edge of discovering a second career. But it was only the first call. Three months after we returned home, the phone rang again. And this time, I was truly unprepared.

"Mel, this is Becky Williams with World Medical Mission in Boone, North Carolina. . . ."

First there were questions. She asked about South Korea. And she asked about our trip home. Then Becky wanted to know something else.

"Mel, I wanted to ask you what you have planned for this next June and July?"

I knew another overseas trip was out. By June the surgery schedule would look like a page from a telephone directory. Every space would be filled. With school out and so many people traveling, there would probably be a heavy load of trauma patients due to driving accidents. After being gone six weeks, my partners would expect me to be on call for a solid week.

"I imagine June and July will be a little full, Becky. But what do you have in mind?"

"There's a hospital in western Kenya where we need you." For the next twenty minutes I listened to a description of the country I had visited but never really got to know. My pen couldn't keep up with the images Becky described. The words crackled as I pressed the ear piece to my head, trying to inch myself closer to this country, this Kenya.

"It's called Tenwek Hospital. There's a collection of modest, cement block buildings, with an operating room, X-ray facility, and even a small pharmacy. It is a remote outpost for over 300,000 people spread out over the hills of western Kenya. Patients walk barefoot for hours, sometimes days, to see a doctor, Mel. Step into a ward and you will see two or three people sharing a bed. Some sleep under the bed.

"There are some very sick people. Children with measles. Not the kind you stay at home from school with and expect a happy get-well card from grandma and grandpa. Are you ready to treat measles that bring on encephalitis and reach epidemic scope? You will see malaria that confines young mothers and

healthy men to bed, before they slowly and quietly die. And, Mel, we will want you to operate. You will probably perform some neurosurgery, your specialty. You will have to do it without the aid of an anesthesiologist. And don't look for handfuls of surgical clamps on the tray. The nearest supply closet is 240 miles down the road in Nairobi.

"You will meet Dr. Ernie Steury, the first missionary physician to arrive at Tenwek in 1959, a humble, gray-haired general practitioner and surgeon. For the first ten of his twenty-five years at Tenwek, he was the only doctor in the compound. Twenty-five years in one place."

I wondered how this Ernie Steury survived. I jotted down the name.

"And you will get to know the Kipsigis, the prominent tribe that makes up ninety percent of Tenwek's patient population. They are a very quiet, soft-spoken people who live in circular huts with grass roofs. The Kipsigis and the Maasai walk up the road to Tenwek every day. You may be the first real doctor many of them have ever seen."

Becky talked. I listened. After I thanked her for calling, I hung up the phone and skated the tip of a ball point pen across a note pad from a drug company. Printed at the top was "Keflex," the name of a drug. I had no way of knowing that antibiotics like this were perpetually in short supply at Tenwek. In fact, they were so limited and so precious that the hospital kept them under lock and key, the way narcotics are handled in U.S. hospitals.

I drew oblong circles that looped up and over the big block printed letters, and always came back to the beginning dot that was growing larger with each round trip of my pen.

I was not prepared for this. Tenwek Hospital didn't need a neurosurgeon for six weeks. They needed more people like Ernie Steury who would give months or years of themselves at a time. What was I avoiding? The chance to start a second career? The hours I would have to put in at work to make up for being gone another month? The explaining I would need to do to my partners who were beginning to wonder what I was up to?

I wish I had known myself. In the rush of the traffic, in the middle of the intersection where doubt and desire meet head on, I prayed. I wondered who and what has the right-of-way in life. My own wishes? A family's collective wish? Perhaps the intent of a God whose purpose you can't fully comprehend at the time? With all of these things deserving lengthy discussions with the Lord, I decided, rather we *all* decided as a family, to visit this world of Tenwek Hospital.

I can't give you a rational reason. The human mind operates over five billion cells. I have performed hundreds of surgeries on the brain, and yet I know I have merely scraped the surface of how this soft mass weighing less than three and a half pounds works to direct a person's thoughts, feelings, and decisions. I can tell you what part of the brain registers taste, and which part affects smell or sight. But I didn't know if mine could find any logical rationale for traveling to a corner of the world to serve people we would probably never really get to know.

With less than three days to go before the flight, we packed everything in eighteen pieces of luggage, including our belongings, antibiotics, shunts for hydrocephalus, surgical towels, orthopedic braces, and surgical instruments. I knew we were above our weight limit. Our suitcases looked vacuum packed, and I was sure they could hold no more. But I was wrong.

Less than seventy-two hours before our plane left, the phone rang.

"Hello, Mel? This is Becky Williams in Boone, North Carolina. I know you're already packed and weighed down with equipment and medical supplies for your trip, but could you possibly take one more thing with you to Kenya?"

"Certainly," I said. "What is it?"

"It's a leg. An artificial leg. For Stanley Cheborge."

Who was Stanley Cheborge?

I knew there were people in the world in need of artificial limbs. I just didn't expect to be the delivery service that would take one halfway around the world to a complete stranger. I didn't have time to learn much about Stanley Cheborge, except that he was a Kipsigis and he was tall. At least I would probably meet him and present him the leg Becky said would arrive at our door the next day.

And it did. Five feet long and nearly a foot square, it was not the kind of toiletry item you tuck in the pocket of a carry-on bag. After the UPS man left, we opened the box and pulled out a long, chocolate-brown leg made of plastic. Stanley had to be a tall man, at least six feet tall.

"I wonder what he looks like," said Elizabeth, surveying the leg that I stood upright in the entry way of our home. Somewhere I had read that Kipsigis are not especially tall. That made Stanley somewhat unusual. We tried to imagine how to pack an artificial leg in such a way that would not raise the curiosity of customs officials after we landed in Nairobi.

Later I remembered how Stanley's eyes opened wide when I told him how Sylvia had sewn a bag out of denim to cover the box containing his leg so customs officials wouldn't notice. I can see him laughing still, this young, vibrant man who was just as tall as I had pictured. And filled with more life than I ever imagined.

FOUR

The way he looked at us told me there would be trouble. "Stay right here. We may be a minute."

The voice of the Kenyan customs official was deep and edged. And he didn't lift an eye off our family's eighteen pieces of luggage. I waited for The Question: "Would you like to tell us what's inside each bag?"

Welcome to Kenya.

I had just spent the past twelve hours in a plastic airline seat, flying from Amsterdam to Nairobi. I didn't look forward to reciting the list of all our family's clothes, toiletries, and dozens of medical supplies to an official stranger who could keep us from entering his country.

At eight o'clock in the morning, the Jomo Kenyatta International Airport in Nairobi was not a place I wanted to be, not with this terse, government agent staring at me, and a line full of weary, foreign travelers waiting behind us.

The customs man now began to intensify his radar-like search. "What is in this?" He pointed to the small column of luggage that sprouted our baggage tags. Laying on top was a long, narrow, blue denim sack.

No, not that bag! Why did he have to ask about that one? The official drilled his index finger into the cloth bag Sylvia had sewn carefully to camouflage the box containing the artificial leg. "I said what is in this?" His words were becoming sharp. Oh, nothing but a five-foot-long artificial limb, I thought. We always take it whenever we go overseas.

"Let's take a look inside." The agent motioned to his assistants. Incredible. It was as if we had taped a Christmas gift tag on the front that said, "Open me first!"

Immediately, a swarm of junior officials converged on the sack as if it were buried treasure. They pulled back the denim carefully and opened the box. Instantly, five chocolate brown toes appeared. Then, slowly, a brown foot, until one smooth perfectly-contoured plastic leg lay exposed on the counter. It was not your ordinary lady's handbag of toiletries. The customs officials recoiled slightly, trying to decide whether to be disappointed or mad. Immediately, I felt the outside of my shirt for the pouch that held my passport. Remember Mel, I had to tell myself, you did this at the request of World Medical Mission for someone named Stanley Cheborge. He desperately needs this leg. So don't ask yourself any more questions such as "Why did we ever put ourselves at risk for someone we don't even know?"

Right now, I wrestled with an even more pressing question: Would we make it safely through customs? Usually, passing through customs and immigration upon entering any other country does not prove to be a problem. Doing so with eighteen duffle bags, boxes, footlockers, suitcases, and a seven-foot long cloth-covered box containing an artificial leg was not usual. This was especially true since most of our luggage also contained assorted medicines, surgical supplies, syringes, needles and other possibly suspicious items. I knew that World Medical Mission would not knowingly send us into a dangerous situation. I also knew that customs control officers could be totally unpredictable. We could be in for trouble! The customs official stared at the naked limb and began stammering in angry Swahili. In one sweeping move of his arm, he grabbed the foot and pulled the leg from its protective cocoon. I knew what was coming. As his frustration moved in slow-motion, I remembered how Sylvia had carefully packed the leg with bags of candies for the missionaries at Tenwek.

The customs official now looked bewildered and proud. He held up the plastic leg with the foot sticking up, like a hunter showing off a rare prize. Instantly, several clear plastic bags of M&M candies fell out of the leg and exploded on the floor. The lobby froze. Heads turned. I looked up and saw camouflaged soldiers on the walkway above tightening the grip on their rifles. Already I could see our entire family sitting in a stuffy immigration office for who knows how many hours.

How do you cover up a thousand M&M candies while they are showering down on cement? I thought of Gene Kelly doing the title number from *Singin' in the Rain*, and I wondered what he would have done to get out of this situation. I imagined him dancing with the leg through customs to a waiting cab, smiling all the way to the curb. Fortunately, I didn't have to call on Gene.

"Sir, let me explain this to you. These people are on an important assignment to help the Kenyan people." The voice belonged to Carol Rape, a missionary coordinator from African Inland Mission, whom we had met only minutes before. This small, unassuming woman suddenly moved and spoke like a confident U.S. State Department diplomat.

"This is not just an artificial leg," Carol proclaimed. "This is part of an important shipment of medical supplies to help the Kenyan people, brought over by American neurosurgeon, Mel Cheatham, and his family."

The Kenyan official looked stunned. He laid the leg down on the counter, and hurriedly asked to see our passports. Then this now-baffled customs chief, still in command, waved his arms with a flurry. "Move these people through! Move them through!" I could hear the stray M&M's crunch under his leather boots as he confidently ushered us through the customs gate. We made our way to the curbside where a truck from Africa Inland Mission waited to receive our luggage, now reduced to only seventeen pieces.

The bag containing the vitally important Pontocaine for administering spinal anesthetics at Tenwek, and some badly needed antibiotics, had been impounded by the customs officer. We could only pray that it would be released as soon as possible, and forwarded to the hospital. Stanley Cheborge's future had been re-tied in its blue denim bag. And I had just rediscovered my pulse.

In the open-air lobby, I felt the cool Nairobi morning surround me. The name of Stanley Cheborge nagged at me like an unwanted R.S.V.P. His leg was just one more piece of baggage we didn't need to carry, unless, of course, he was a government dignitary, someone important Becky Williams had failed to tell us about. When we got to Tenwek, I would be glad to meet him and give him the leg. In fact, I was ready to get it over with. Just give him the leg so I could fully concentrate on the upcoming task of helping sick people feel well again.

I stood on the curb of the loading area with four other weary adults. The artificial limb, even in its box and dressed in jean material, looked genuinely out of place. Carol Rape appeared again, this time to usher us into a waiting vehicle as the driver loaded our luggage into the back. Destination: Wilson Airport on the southern edge of Nairobi, where we would take a small missionary plane to Tenwek Hospital. To get to Wilson, we rode in a Volkswagon micro bus, covered with hundreds of scrapes and dents. The driver laid the blue, oblong sack on top of a small mountain of luggage. He hesitated a moment, unsure of just what he was moving. "It's for a friend," I told him.

The single-engine Cessna he took us to was too small and too light for five adults and a mountain of luggage.

"We could take four of you on board," said the pilot.

"I'll go with Barbara," said Michael, our oldest son. He chose to ride with Barbara Pinkley, a registered nurse from Tenwek who met us at Wilson with a four-wheel-drive vehicle to transport our luggage the last several hundred miles to the hospital. Into her van we loaded all of our luggage and Michael. The sky was clouding over. The wind was up. Michael, who was prone to airsickness, preferred riding nearly seven hours of bumpy roads to ninety up-and-down minutes in the air.

I waved good-bye to the vehicle as it became a speck in the distance. Then I swallowed hard. A single-engine Cessna was not my definition of comfort. After meeting the pilot it should have been. While squeezing himself into the cockpit, he revealed he had made a comfortable living flying a private Lear jet for years. Then, he said he gave it all up, and had chosen instead to fly as a missionary pilot, because he said he wanted to serve the Lord. He didn't mind covering miles of uninhabited earth, risking his own life daily to take people like us to the tiny places in Africa the map makers had ignored.

"In the event we go down," he told us, "this is what you will need to do. . . ." I fastened the seat belt tight around my waist and wiped the sweat from my upper lip. I was trusting a man I had just barely met with my family's physical safety. When he finished his emergency instructions, he said, "Let us pray." And in that tiny cabin I remembered the One a missionary pilot trusts for his fragile plane and human cargo.

The plane sprinted down the narrow runway, broke free from the ground and climbed into the clouds. Yet, I could not separate myself from the Kenya I saw below me. For the next ninety minutes, the earth was a speckled swarm of green and brown. The western rim of the Great Rift Valley rose up under the wing. Although the altimeter read 7,500 feet, the approaching mountain peaks of the Mau Escarpment looked disturbingly close. My world became buried in clouds. We banked left, and outside the window I saw an endless green carpet emerge. It was the Great Mau Forest, miles and miles of tall trees that give way to cultivated hillsides, then the flatlands of the Maasai Mara and eventually the Serengetti Plain of Tanzania.

Then, from my left in the cockpit, came the announcement: "There it is," the pilot pointed. "Tenwek Hospital."

I strained to see above the instrument panel. Through the invisible whirl of the propeller blade, I saw a cluster of buildings appear on the top of a wooded hill. Toward the bottom, a dark, muddy river curled through what seemed to be a valley. A waterfall near the hospital spouted white spray and drew my attention back to a collection of metal and tile rooftops.

Where was I? On the National Geographic map of eastern Africa, Tenwek was not even a town, but merely an unseen outpost near names like Kisumu, Kericho and Bomet, where a grass landing strip grew wider as the plane descended. There were no buildings in sight, not even a wind-sock.

Looking down from 3,000 feet, Tenwek was no bigger than a pinpoint. On a global map of medical missions, however, the hospital's name and reputation with the people of western Kenya couldn't have been larger. Some forty years earlier, in 1942, Tenwek existed only as an idea, when the District Commissioner from Kericho proposed to the World Gospel Mission that they open a hospital at Chemagel, twenty-five miles from Tenwek. That year, *Call to Prayer*, the World Gospel Mission magazine, carried a plea: "We have had many reasons to put in a claim for a resident physician here at Tenwek during the past twelve months. . . . We do not feel that it is too early to ask our friends at home and our Father in heaven to meet this keenly felt need."

Seventeen years later, with his wife, Sue, Dr. Ernest Steury arrived from Berne, Indiana, as Tenwek's first physician. What started out as a thirty-two-bed hospital was now a teeming medical outpost.

I had experienced many runway approaches before, mostly riding in large commercial jets. But none like the one now beneath me. The pilot made a low pass over the hospital and mission grounds, waggling the wings up and down to signal our arrival. I didn't know it at the time, but it was the only way he could make contact with the people below. As the plane dipped and swung down over the ground, I could see large numbers of people gathering outside the hospital.

The Cessna climbed and flew northwest. Five miles later the Bomet landing strip was in view. We made what felt like a 180-degree turn. The pilot then made the approach to land. As the plane descended to thirty feet above the grass, I felt the cabin rise up under my feet. At full throttle, the plane roared nearly the length of the grass strip before rising just enough to clear the tall trees at the end of the strip. "That's to frighten the animals who might be nearby or grazing on the runway," the pilot said as he circled back. By now my nerves were flying first class.

We were seconds from earth. I looked down and noticed my hands were gripped tightly around my camera case. Suddenly, a loud, shrill horn penetrated the cabin. Warning! The aircraft was now in stall position. I peered out the side window as we rode a bed of air for longer than I could count. Then a sudden shake. The plane's wheels hit the ground, bouncing, bouncing, then finally touching down for good. The trees and fields outside my window jiggled to a brief halt. Then everything spun around as the pilot taxied the plane to the center of the grassy clearing. And we stopped.

"Watch your head as you climb out," he said. It was a warning I was glad to hear, still awake after twenty-four straight hours. I followed the pilot through the cramped doorway. Then I stepped onto the wing strut in my final descent to the spongy earth.

First, I helped Sylvia from the plane. Then Elizabeth. Then Robert. Next, I had to see where we were. My head turned in a full circle like a weathervane. What happened next still throws shivers up my back. From across the landscape of hillside and forest I saw thin, dark figures walking toward us. One by one, they started to appear, as if from nowhere, men, women, and small children in tattered clothing all coming closer.

They approached in silence. At first it was only a scattered few. But the number swelled to several handfuls until there were probably a hundred. And what I will never forget is that they surrounded the four of us without saying a word. We must have stood in the shade of the airplane's wing for fifteen minutes or so. It was still, and it was eerie. And yet I felt the strange assurance of knowing we were totally safe.

How long would this go on? The silence was broken by what sounded like an approaching vehicle that had left a dusty road and was now crossing a ditch. A green Land Rover swung onto the grass strip and rumbled to a stop next to the plane. Out stepped a white-skinned young woman with red hair and a confident smile. "My name is Jody Stevens," she said as she extended her hand to shake each of ours, before proceeding to help unload our hand luggage. I was overwhelmed by her warmth and we started chatting like old friends, almost before the car's engine turned over. Now, all around the vehicle, the Kenyans stood, surrounding us much like they had the plane.

I looked down at a bronze-skinned boy whose forehead came only to the bottom of the window. He looked up, smiling, and his eyes said, "Please stay." I reached out to shake his hand, and set off a chain reaction. Dozens of outstretched arms and hands of all sizes suddenly came at us. They were accompanied by wide, toothy smiles, but still not a word was spoken. These were the Kipsigis I had read about in books, strangely quiet and respectful of the white man and his party that had dropped out of the sky. With a few goodbyes we waved as we drove off down the rough, bumpy road. As I looked back over my shoulder I saw these gentle faces disappear into billows of dust and the grinding of gears.

We moved through the foreign countryside and a new world paraded past my eyes—lush, rolling hillsides separated by low hedge rows with clumps of tall trees. Thinly-clad children walking cows, which our hosts told us, supplied a family's milk. How long would it be, I wondered, before I noticed that the boy lying on the operating table in front of me was the same child I had seen walking home with his cows?

The road curled into a collection of corrugated metal rooftops. And suddenly there was a sign: *"TENWEK HOSPITAL. WE TREAT—JESUS HEALS."* We passed the entrance gate and there, along each side of the road, I could see crowds of black-skinned people, lined up outside the hospital.

"They look like they're waiting," I said to Jody who was driving.

"They've been waiting, some for hours, just to see a doctor. Some have been waiting all day. They start gathering out front at the outpatient clinic as early as six o' clock in the morning— depending on how many miles they have to walk.

"Many who don't see a doctor today will come back tomorrow. Time is no factor for our patients. What's a few more hours when you've lived the same simple, basic life for hundreds of years?

"We usually have no more than five doctors here at Tenwek. They treat the medical needs of over 300,000 people who live throughout the surrounding hills. Our daily census runs about 250 in the hospital. Our doctors and staff commonly put in twelve- and fourteen-hour days, and the work is never done. It's a matter of doing as much as we can, then picking up where we left off when the sun comes up again."

I saw the face of a Kipsigis woman with a child on her back. The strain on the woman's face needed no translation. While this picture rolled past me, Franklin Graham's words reverberated in my head: "We're not looking for doctors who want a vacation. We want people who will come and work." As we passed the woman and her baby, the pain I saw on her face remained.

The Land Rover came to a stop on the lawn of a small house with a plaque that said "Steury's." I stepped out and took a deep breath. Flowering bushes were everywhere. One more sensation flooding my brain. And another was on the way. I looked down a small dirt road and saw a middle aged white man. He was wearing jeans, a sport shirt, a white hospital coat and a grin. By the time he was within arm's reach, I had already started walking toward him.

"Hi, I'm Marty Graber."

"Mel Cheatham. Good to meet you."

"Are you hungry?" he asked. "We've got lunch waiting for you." He saw the effects of traveling through ten time zones written on my face.

"Can I have a cup of coffee?" I asked.

"Black, or with cream?"

I liked this man right away. I soon began to learn why. We walked down the path to a plain-looking, cinder-block building.

He opened the front door and we walked into a living room that felt like a piece of the Midwest. Inside a woman reached out and grabbed our hands.

"Hi, I'm Ann Graber. We've been waiting for you." In minutes we were sitting at their dining table, like old neighbors catching up on the last fifty years.

"We're Hoosiers," Ann said. "Indiana was the only world we ever knew, until we came to Tenwek." Marty and Ann Graber seemed as genuine and basic as the furniture dotting their home. Strong. Sincere. And comfortable right from the start. There was nothing fancy about their speech, or how they offered us seconds on soup. For them, hospitality was as natural as pouring coffee.

Our conversation circled the table. Sylvia, Elizabeth, Robert and I fielded the questions like pop flies in a summer softball game. Where did we grow up? What made our coming to Africa a family decision? Didn't someone tell you, Mel, that anesthesiologists are almost extinct in this part of Africa? Do you know what you're getting yourself into?

In a state of jet lag, I talked on, covering over my short-term memory of airports and schedules, with another swallow of coffee. Then, as I was describing the small dispensary of medications we had brought with us, Marty broke in.

"Do you have Stanley's leg?"

"Yes," I said. "It's coming out with Barbara Pinkley, who's driving from Nairobi with our oldest son, Michael."

His name had come up again. Why? Why so much interest in this Stanley Cheborge? Had I missed something in the phone call from Becky Williams? Was he a government official? An educator? Maybe a foreign ambassador?

"Of course we're all looking forward to meeting him," I said to Marty. At the same time, I knew I just wanted to see where my family and I were going to live for the next six weeks.

And before I unloaded any artificial leg, I was going to make sure Michael arrived safely with Barbara. Those were the priorities. Son. Unpack. Sleep. And somewhere down the list, artificial leg, in that order.

Marty rose from his chair and pulled a ring of keys out of his front pocket.

"I'm going to go get Stanley and bring him back tonight so you can examine him."

Marty started moving toward the front door. By now, the curiosity that had been percolating inside me for weeks bubbled over.

"Tell me, Marty, just who is this Stanley Cheborge?"

Marty seemed surprised. "I'm sorry. I was sure you knew."

"All I know is that we put an artificial leg on the plane and it's riding across Kenya at this moment. And that its recipient is someone who's gotten more attention in the past several days than any one of our children."

I looked at Marty. What did he know that I didn't? We sat back down and he began to talk. He told us how he and Ann had come to know a Kipsigis tribesman named Stanley Cheborge, how he had walked into their lives unexpectedly one day and had captured their attention in a way no Kenyan, no other person, ever had. He told us how there had been so much hope to begin with. And then things began to turn ugly. As Marty told more of the story, his voice grew quiet. Then his words began to dissolve into a handful of dangling questions about Stanley and what now awaited him.

By now I knew something, and that was why this missionary doctor, barraged from dawn to dusk with a patient list that had no end, was going to drop everything for four hours and drive twenty miles of terrible roads to the edge of Stanley's mud-walled hut and bring him back to Tenwek. Even though there was more to the story than we had time for, I knew Marty had no choice. And neither did I. I would have to meet this Kenyan. And if Marty came back late, I would wait up, just to see Stanley Cheborge.

I took another swallow from my cup. The simple luxury of sitting in one place, especially after bouncing in the air for two days is a foreign event, especially for a doctor. When you're used to looking at life from behind an operating mask, under unforgiving lights and the self-imposed pressure to make your next incision absolutely perfect, you forget how to relax. And that had caused some questions. Was I ever going to jump off the treadmill of work and find the time to take inventory of my own heart? What was I really doing in Kenya? I knew the starting gun would be going off very soon, and my coffee would spill over into the next six weeks of intense demands. Just the chance to catch my breath was all I wanted.

"Dr. Graber, Dr. Graber! You come please? Someone need help right away."

I looked over at the Grabers' front door, swung partially open. A short Kenyan woman dressed in a green uniform stood there nervously, her head leaning in part way. Marty looked at me. Without saying a word we both knew exactly what would happen next. Before I could take another sip, the Kipsigis had found my beeper. It was time to go to work.

I stood up, hugged Sylvia briefly, along with Elizabeth and Robert, thanked Ann Graber, and stepped into the world of Tenwek Hospital. Marty and I moved up the hill to the main buildings, past clusters of Kenyan women holding babies and men standing or sitting silently. All of them now turned to stare at the white men walking past them. I walked into a small room and found a change of surgical greens. Marty showed me the operating room, just one door away. In the space of a few goodbyes, he was out the door to go pick up Stanley Cheborge.

I was on my own. I adjusted my surgical mask and peered through a small window of the operating theater where a surgery was already underway. Less than two hours ago my sweaty hands were feeling the metal cocoon of a single engine plane. Now, I was moments away from plunging them into a pair of rubber gloves that would hold a suture, a needle, a clamp, and the outcome of a surgery I would help perform.

"Hi, I'm Bob Wesche. Scrub up and come on in. I can use some help."

His surgical mask covered most of his face, but not the warm, friendly eyes of this prematurely graying man looking at me. Dr. Bob Wesche spoke as if I had been his partner for years. After scrubbing my hands with surgical soap, I stood across the table from this man and got my first glimpse of surgery at Tenwek: a young Kenyan woman with a ruptured appendix that had caused a large abscess and now needed to be drained. It was a common procedure I had performed many times. But that had been twenty-five years ago. Though the surgery seemed routine, the patient deserved as much care as if she were undergoing the most specialized operation I had ever performed. She was someone's daughter. She was a person whose life mattered.

As Dr. Wesche and I worked together, I noticed his hands. They moved with the delicacy and confidence of a skilled surgeon. Thousands of miles beyond the borders of the revered American medical community, I found a new respect for my profession in a new colleague who was not afraid to share his knowledge with me.

"See that small worm crawling about on the surface of the intestine?" Bob said, pointing to the organ. "That is a positive Tenwek sign!" He explained that most patients in rural Kenya had intestinal parasites. When the intestine was opened, such as this woman's was with a ruptured appendix, you could see the parasites crawling about the inside of the abdominal cavity.

"This woman will be all right, once we've given her a course of antibiotics and medication for the intestinal parasites," he said. "Trouble is, the people here have not been in the habit of boiling their drinking water, and they get parasitic infections all over again. Dr. David Stevens, our medical director, has started a very active program of community health training which will teach the people, like this woman, the importance of boiling their water before drinking or cooking with it."

In those opening moments of surgery, I came face-to-face with Third World medicine. Bob's student was an eager, somewhat jet-lagged, veteran neurosurgeon on the eve of doing his first general surgery in twenty-five years. For the past six months I had been reading operative dictations, notes of specific procedures from my former surgeries, and I had reviewed textbooks to refresh my knowledge. Now Bob Wesche and I were turning pages in the real thing.

Our first surgery lasted only thirty minutes, and I was ready for more. As we sutured up the patient's abdomen, Bob began to ask questions:

How long had we been able to spend with the Grabers?

Did Marty say just when he planned to return?

And of course he must have told you about Stanley, didn't he?

"We've wondered exactly what's causing the pain in his hip and leg," Bob said. "There's the distinct possibility it's the result of a ruptured disc in his lower spine. Maybe the new artificial leg you brought with you might give him some relief."

Right now the leg was riding across southwestern Kenya with Barbara Pinkley and Michael. In several hours it would be dark. As curious as I was to meet this one-legged stranger, I had become preoccupied with other thoughts. Where was my son?

Could I ever find our living quarters in the dark? Did someone at Tenwek have a flashlight? And what on earth was a talented surgeon like Bob Wesche doing out here in such a remote land when, obviously, he could be teaching in a university surgical training program in the U.S.? How had God called him to this corner of the world, along with a neurosurgeon from California?

The surgery took us only another few minutes to complete. After we were done, Bob led me on his rounds to the female ward. He talked and I listened, trying to comprehend how many sick individuals could be packed, bed frame-to-bed frame, along two walls that stretched for seventy-five feet.

Do you see this woman just recovering from a bowel obstruction?

Here is a lady who just had her thyroid removed under local anesthesia. She had a large goiter.

Look at this young girl. She had skin grafted onto thirty percent of her body that was burned when she fell into a cooking fire in her family's hut.

Here is a young mother who is doing well after a cesarean section.

And here is a lady living day-by-day after an operation for cancer of the pancreas. She experiences great pain. All I could do was sew her up again.

Every woman we saw spoke in a meek, low-pitched voice, and just about every woman dropped her head and turned partially to the side as she spoke. I wondered if this were out of false shame, or cultural obligation. All I saw were sick, brave individuals cared for by a talented surgeon working with severely limited equipment and supplies.

The call came for Bob and me to return to surgery. For the next few hours it was one operation after another, and Bob Wesche performed each as if the patient were his only one. With each surgery my respect for him grew. He had no specialists to call on, no clinic to consult, no other resident surgeon to relieve him. I looked over at Bob, immersed in the operation, and I thought, *Who would I turn to when I operated on that first patient at Tenwek and realized I was the only doctor who could make the critical decision?*

The question wouldn't go away, as we continued to operate through the afternoon. I could tell Bob Wesche was getting tired, so I finished one of the abdominal operations in order for him to drop out and do some other work. After closing the incision, I wanted to find out where he had gone. I found him sitting in the supply room where they keep sterile instruments. He was busy surveying the list of surgeries that needed to be done the next day.

"We have twenty-three operations to do tomorrow," he said, as I sat down opposite him. "Things have piled up a bit with Dr. Carlos Somoza away on holiday this past week. Mel, why don't you pick out those operations you feel you can do, and I'll take the rest. That way we can run two operating rooms tomorrow. If you need some help, I can always break scrub in my room and come over and give you a hand, briefly."

It seemed like a generous offer. We looked at the list together and divided up the surgeries. Finally, I saw one case that, to make things equal, should have been mine. It was an orthopedic case, a young boy with osteomyelitis, an infection in the bone of his right leg. Bob saw it too.

"You take that one," he said.

"I don't know, Bob," I quickly replied. "It's been a long time since I've done an operation like that."

He looked up at me, unfazed. "The anatomy hasn't changed."

"All right," I said, "I'll take it."

Our break ended, and within a few minutes, we were back in the operating theater, looking at a new patient, a new problem. Time was running away with the afternoon. We were in between surgeries when a face appeared in the doorway. It was Marty Graber.

"Stanley's in his room and he's waiting to see you."

Bob Wesche glanced up. "Let's finish up here and go to see him." Within minutes, we walked outside, past the outpatient area where men and women sat on benches, still waiting to be seen by the surgeon. I was sure the first thing he would ask me would be about the artificial leg, one I didn't have to give. If he was like so many other patients, Stanley would probably get right into describing his pain. Being a Kipsigis, perhaps with little grasp of English, he would need some coaxing. I was prepared to nudge him along.

As Bob and I approached his room, I opened the door and peered into a dimly lit space. There, I saw a long-legged, dark-skinned man stretched out on a small, narrow bed. His upper torso was supported on one elbow. As I stepped into the room, I caught sight of his face and a wide smile.

"Welcome, my name is Stanley!"

The words were deep and the voice was big.

"You must be Dr. Cheatham. I'm sure that you are very weary from your long journey. Please come and sit down."

Right away I knew he was different. I can't tell you how I knew this, but it was true. His English surprised me. This was not the typical, quiet Kipsigis man I had seen waiting outside the hospital. His words were crisp and bright. Where he had learned the language, I didn't know.

He seemed to have limitless hope. They say there are people, who, by their personal magnetism, can fill a room. Stanley Cheborge was one of these persons. Even while bedridden, lying on his side, what came from his eyes and his words pulled me in. And wouldn't let go. There was no self-pity, no longing for attention, no mention of his illness. Instead of focusing on his own pain, he wanted to know about me.

I wanted to talk to him, find out who he was, but something held me back. Bob Wesche moved to the side of his bed. The friendship and trust between them was obvious as they talked about how Stanley was feeling. I watched as the two men talked; Bob in his hunched-over posture, nodding quietly as Stanley described the rushes of pain he could not control.

In the moments that followed, while the two talked, I tried to piece together that story Marty Graber had started to tell me a few hours ago.

About ten years ago, while running, Stanley began experiencing an ache in his left knee. At first he thought it was just a muscle pull. But a month later, while playing soccer, Stanley suddenly felt and heard his left leg break. He was taken to Tenwek where Dr. Ernest Steury examined him and found a tumor just below the knee. As a life-saving act, the leg was amputated several days later.

In recent months, a new problem had developed, an unexplainable pain that now constantly throbbed in Stanley's lower back and radiated down his right leg.

Marty's brief yet revealing overview led me to think Stanley might just have a ruptured disc. Stanley's cancer had been ten years ago. I found it unlikely, though not impossible, that the cancer could be back. I knew he had used a poorly fitting prosthesis, and that walking several miles each day on craggy, terrible roads could give anyone a ruptured disc. In fact just bouncing up and down for twenty miles in Marty's vehicle had no doubt only punctuated his pain.

A ruptured disc was not out of the question, but I needed to get a clearer picture of the actual problem. I had successfully operated on many patients who were now able to walk and live comfortably without the pain of a ruptured disc. For the moment I felt I could help this young man who obviously had a great impact on people.

Marty had told me that Stanley had come to Tenwek as a patient and then two years later had returned as a student at Tenwek High School, where it would be easier for him to get around while still using a stick. During this time he developed a very close family relationship with Dr. and Mrs. Steury, so close in fact, he called them "Mum and Dad." Stanley couldn't have been more surprised than the day Dr. Steury found an artificial leg in a shipment of medical supplies. It fit him perfectly and Stanley was thrilled. He could walk more normally now, but the leg was white. Dr. Steury suggested they get him some long pants, but Stanley said he could not wear long pants. He'd been elected chairman of the Christian Union and it was very important that he follow all the school's rules—including wearing the short pants required by the uniform. When the headmaster agreed to allow Stanley to wear long pants, Stanley was very happy. He could walk on two legs and keep the white one covered, and he wouldn't be breaking the rules. At the school Stanley began to spend hours with patients, listening, praying, sharing with them about how the Lord had given him strength and hope even in the darkest of situations.

The patients trusted Stanley because he could relate to them out of his own pain. When they met Stanley they met a person, a man with one leg, who lived with joy and confidence, and who believed God was always walking with him.

"In Stanley you'll see a strength, the kind of character that will make him a major leader someday," Marty had said. "And I know, Mel, whatever you do for Stanley will change not only his life, but more lives than you or I can imagine." And, as Marty talked, I looked over at the bed where Bob Wesche talked with the lanky Kipsigis man, and I wondered where Stanley Cheborge would be three years, ten years, thirty years from now.

I could hear Dr. Wesche and Stanley talking about his leg. I heard the name "Dr. Cheatham" several times and words about how I, as a neurosurgeon, would be able to explain the pain that now throbbed continuously in Stanley's lower back and radiated down his only leg.

"What do you think, doctor?" Bob Wesche looked over at me with his rhetorical question that signaled it was time to leave.

"I think we need to come back tomorrow and find out how to help our young patient," I said, glancing past Bob over to Stanley.

"I know God has brought you to Tenwek for a reason, to heal me," Stanley called back. "Tomorrow, when you examine me, there will just be the three of us," he said.

"Three?" I asked.

"You. Me. And Him," Stanley said pointing upward.

He spoke with the faith of a child who lived with tears inside, but chose not to shed them. To reach Tenwek, Stanley had ridden in a combi-van, an international cousin to the old Volkswagon Microbus. He had bounced over twenty miles of terrible dirt roads with a nagging companion, a still-unexplained disease in the lower spine that now caused him constant pain. Yet, as I said good-bye for the first time that night, I saw a warmth in his eyes as real as the aching in his bones.

When Bob Wesche and I left Stanley's room, it was pitch black outside, and the sky held a million stars. We used a small flashlight to cut a path out of the darkness down the hill. We chatted like old friends, and discovered we were, in fact, the same age. I not only felt his company as a physician and as a Christian, I knew I would value his presence if and when I operated on Stanley Cheborge.

We reached the bottom of the hill and I prepared to go in an opposite direction to the guest quarters.

"If I seem a bit overwhelmed by all I've experienced today, it's only because I *am*," I said. Then I asked Bob, "You don't think I will feel any pressure if it's necessary for me to operate on Stanley as my first neurosurgery patient at Tenwek, do you, Bob? It seems to me he's the most popular man in the area."

"For a man whose been through as many time zones as surgical gloves in the past seventy-two hours, I can assure you that you are exactly where you need to be," Bob said. He paused for a moment and then looked right at me.

"I am also absolutely convinced the Lord will use your talents and work through you as you treat Stanley. Whatever becomes of him, his problem with pain, his life, nothing will change this truth."

Bob turned to walk to his quarters. But his comment remained with me as I felt my way through the dark to find our family's guest quarters for the first time. One man's confidence had spoken to another man's concern. And I could hear both voices as I walked along listening to the crickets. I suddenly felt a very long way from home. It all seemed a little strange, because for the moment, I didn't know where home was.

The sound of a vehicle broke through my thoughts. Without turning around I saw my shadow lengthen as the beam of approaching headlights hit my back. A vehicle rolled up and behind the window I spotted the faces of Barbara Pinkley and my son, Michael. Both were covered with dust as they climbed out, tired yet still intact after what turned out to be an eight-hour drive from Nairobi. I looked inside. It was all there, sixteen pieces of luggage and one long denim-covered box with a leg inside of it.

A few minutes later I lay stretched out on the bed next to Sylvia. I had every reason to feel spent, and totally grateful. For an entire family that had arrived safely in a strange new world. For the pillow under my head. And for this night of quiet that wrapped itself around all my many thoughts.

FIVE

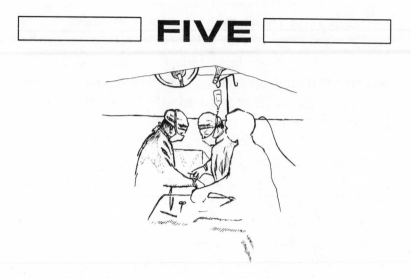

Early the next morning, Michael and I carried Stanley's artificial leg up the hill from our guest quarters to the hospital. Its final destination was now only a few yards away. With Michael's arms under one end, and mine around the other, we walked up to Stanley's door. As I looked through the open doorway, I could see him reading his large, black Bible.

"Good morning, Stanley," I said, as we made our way into the small room.

"Ah, Dr. Cheatham, you have returned to see me," Stanley replied. "And what is it that you have? Can it be the new leg which you have brought me from America?"

"Yes, Stanley, it is the artificial leg."

A grin spread across his face. "This new leg may be the answer to my problem," he said. "Now I should be able to walk again, without pain, and be prepared to continue the work which the Lord has called me to do."

"Before you try to walk with your new leg," I said, "I'll need to examine your back and good leg." In my mind I reviewed the pieces of information I already knew about the bright, young man stretched out on the bed.

The long years of abnormal strain on his lower spine might have caused a ruptured disc. This could be placing pressure on his sciatic nerve, causing the pain to radiate down his leg. Possibly, and remotely, the pain might be related to his previous bone cancer. However, X-rays to date had not shown any evidence of this.

The examination took no more than five minutes, but it confirmed my basic suspicion: Stanley had a pinched nerve. But I discovered something else. The numbness in his leg extended further than I would expect from a ruptured disc. And that made me worry.

I wanted to order a CT scan of the lumbar spine. This high-tech, computerized tomography, a diagnostic X-ray study, would allow me to literally look inside Stanley's spine without even touching him. But Tenwek Hospital did not have equipment nearly sophisticated enough. I would have to settle for the tired, old, basic X-ray machine with which to take pictures of Stanley's spine.

"Stanley, I want to take you over to the X-ray room later this morning and do a special test called a myelogram."

"What is that, Dr. Cheatham?"

"I will inject a solution that I brought from America directly into the spinal fluid sac within your spine. I will do this through a long needle. Then X-rays can be taken which will help to show what is going on inside your spine."

Stanley looked directly at me. "Dr. Cheatham, I know God has brought you here to heal my body, and I have placed myself in your hands. I have put my total faith and trust in the Lord. Please do whatever you feel you must do to help me."

"I will, Stanley. Please be assured that we will do all that we can to help you."

It was time to go. Michael and I excused ourselves to make morning rounds with Bob Wesche. It meant seeing some fifty hospitalized patients and perhaps a dozen more outpatients during the day. In addition, Bob and I had twenty-three operations scheduled between us—more than we would possibly be able to do. Those we couldn't operate on that day would have to be rescheduled for another day, adding to an agenda that was probably already full.

Around mid-morning, while Dr. Wesche and I operated, I heard my name being called. "Dr. Cheatham! Please come to the X-ray room between operations." Solomon, the chief X-ray technician, wanted us to see Stanley. Five minutes later, I came into the room and saw Stanley lying in a prone position on the X-ray table. I cleaned his lower back with surgical prep solution and proceeded to insert the four-inch-long spinal needle until clear spinal fluid started to flow out. Then I injected the Pantopaque solution directly into Stanley's spinal fluid sac. Solomon took the X-ray that would allow me to see more clearly what was causing Stanley's pain.

Michael and I talked to him as he lay on his stomach. "Stanley," I said, "if the myelogram shows an abnormality, we can plan to go ahead with surgery. Tomorrow morning we would do a laminectomy—an operation on the lower spine."

"I have placed myself in your care," Stanley said. "I am ready for whatever is necessary to restore me to health."

Solomon came back, holding up smoky X-ray pictures to the naked lightbulb above. I could make out the dense, white shadow of the Pantopaque within the spinal fluid sac. In the lower spinal canal the dye came to an abrupt halt, as if something were squeezing the fluid sac containing the nerves to the lower half of Stanley's body.

"The study is abnormal," I told Stanley. "What we see here is abnormal. It could be a very large ruptured disc, as we have suspected." I held the X-ray film in front of him so he could see what I was describing.

"We need to operate on you tomorrow morning." The surgery was absolutely necessary. And we both knew it.

"Dr. Werner is coming." Solomon's quiet, respectful voice caught me off guard.

"Who is Dr. Werner?" I asked.

"He is a radiologist, and he should be on the airplane which just flew over us."

I couldn't believe what I was hearing. I thought to myself, *What is this? I do a myelogram and wish there were a radiologist to look at the X-ray with me. Then Solomon calmly announces to me that a radiologist is landing.* It had to be the quickest answer to prayer, ever.

Without warning, Michael stuck his head in the door. "Dad, there's an emergency cesarean section that needs to be done." I rushed to the operating theater remembering that Bob Wesche had told me earlier I would be doing C-sections at Tenwek, and that he would help me.

I got to the room and saw Bob give the mother-to-be a spinal anesthetic. Quickly, he lowered her down from a sitting position onto her back. Then he checked the level of ascending numbness as it moved from her feet upward to her lower rib cage. Bob raised the head of the operating table and asked, "Mama, ngwan?" ("Mother, do you feel pain here?") as he pinched the skin of her abdomen. After he confirmed she could no longer move her legs, we both moved quickly to the sinks outside the operating theater to scrub our hands and arms for the required seven minutes. We gowned, gloved ourselves, then draped the patient with the gravid abdomen protruding high like a huge, brown mound through the opening in the sterile sheets.

Bob handed me the knife. With a long, downward sweep, I made the incision from the bellybutton to the pubic bone, then opened the transparent peritoneum lining the abdominal cavity to expose the uterus. With the incision complete, amniotic fluid gushed forth. Reaching inside the uterus my right hand swept deeply along the black hair of the baby's head, then gently pulled upward, as Bob pushed on the abdomen from above.

Out came the head, then one shoulder and arm followed by another. The small pelvis and legs followed. A new baby entered the world still attached to his mother's lifeblood by the umbilical cord. Swiftly, Bob cut and clamped the cord as I suctioned the mucous and fluid from the baby's mouth, just in time for him to take a deep breath of room air, open his eyes, and cry.

There was no time to admire this tiny miracle cradled in my hands. I handed the baby to the midwife who waited with a sterile towel outstretched. Bob and I now turned our attention to the mother's briskly bleeding uterus. With the umbilical cord and the placenta expelled, I injected a small amount of Pitocin that caused the uterus to contract. Then I began to quickly sew the gaping opening in the birth canal and uterus back together.

I glanced over and saw the broad smile on the face of the mother as she was shown her eleventh child, and seventh son. It was a happy moment, one that would have been worth making the entire trip to Kenya. I did some fast stitching while Bob took off his surgical gown and gloves and crossed the scrub room to begin the next surgery in the adjoining operating theater. This pace continued throughout the day.

It was late afternoon when a young-looking couple from Clarkston, Washington, opened the swinging doors of the operating room and peered inside. "Hello," I said.

"Hi, we're Les and Sara Werner," said the man. "We just arrived a few hours ago, and I have been reading over some of the X-rays done today."

"It's nice meeting you," I replied.

Les went on. "Mel, I've looked at the myelogram film on Stanley Cheborge. With the bright light, I see what may be some bone erosion in the sacrum. This is not really definite because the X-ray picture is so smoky, but it raises the question of a possible tumor."

Immediately I stopped what I was doing, then took a deep breath. "Oh no." I looked up at Les and Sara. "I've considered the possibility that the problem might be due to recurrence of the osteogenic sarcoma, which Stanley had in his left leg ten years ago, but I've tried to ignore this as a strong possibility. What you're telling me is not good news."

"Sara is a neurologist, and she'll be happy to examine Stanley and offer her opinion, if you wish."

"By all means," I said.

I refocused my attention on the operation I'd been so engrossed in a moment before. My heart felt heavy as I thought what the picture on the new myelogram film might mean to Stanley. I thought of the added challenge that would face me the next morning when I operated on him. I took another deep breath, keeping all my thoughts inside.

It was dark when we finally finished operating on the last of about sixteen patients. Then, there were surgical outpatients to see. Finally Michael and I found our way to Stanley's hospital room. I could tell he was in good spirits.

"Dr. Cheatham, I welcome you back!" Stanley exclaimed. "And have you any news about the operation which you will do tomorrow to relieve my pain?"

"Yes, Stanley. I have more information to give you about your X-ray pictures. Dr. Werner is a radiologist, and he believes he can see some signs of possible tumor in the bone of your spine. Therefore, it may be a tumor and not a disc that is pressing on your spinal nerves and causing your pain and numbness."

As I spoke, the warm, confident smile faded from the young man's face, and the up-turned corners of his mouth dropped into an expression of disbelief. A long pause filled the small room. After a silence that seemed to speak louder than his rich, deep voice, Stanley looked up. "Doctor Cheatham, can you not operate on my spine and remove this tumor? Can you not relieve my suffering and restore my health?"

"Stanley, in your case, if you have a tumor and it is malignant, this will not be possible. We can do surgery. If we find a tumor, we can biopsy it. But if it is a cancer, surgical cure is not possible. With biopsy and partial removal of the tumor," I continued, "radiation therapy and chemotherapy in Nairobi might be possible. And in that case the outlook might be improved."

These last few words were a small concession to the sharp reality Stanley was facing. The news of a possible tumor must have been doubly painful to him because he not only heard my words, he now had to repeat them to his family in their native tongue. Only Annah, his wife, understood English. As she listened to Stanley translate his cancer into Kipsigis for the benefit of his brothers, I could see her tremble.

When Stanley had finished explaining the bad news, he dropped his head, and his eyes stared right through the floor. Stanley's brothers looked directly at me, their emotionless faces betraying none of the pain that must have filled their hearts. Annah seemed unable to look at me, as if wanting to hide the hurt that everyone could see.

I felt compelled to try to offer some hope. Yet, I still had to be honest. "Stanley, it may not be a tumor in your spine. It could be a ruptured disc, and this would not be a bad thing. Let's wait and see what it is, and pray that it will be something we can treat successfully." Stanley suddenly looked upward and stared into my eyes. He could see the truth. Without saying a word, his look told me he knew the odds were not in his favor; the operative findings would bring bad news. Again, he dropped his head in despair.

Something in the corner of my eye moved. I looked over at the doorway and there stood two men. As if responding to a beeperless pager, Marty Graber and Bob Wesche walked into the room and saw Stanley in his bed, silent and sullen. Immediately the two could feel a collective grief in the room that had no words. They saw a patient and a friend facing the immensity of his own situation. For more minutes than I could count he kept staring down, as if expecting to find the happy ending of a story that didn't exist.

Then, while the people in the room looked on, Stanley lifted his head and said, "Dr. Graber, please pray for me."

Marty Graber took a step forward and prayed for God to extend His blessing to Stanley and his family. He asked God to be present in the midst of their physical suffering and fear. And he prayed for God to bring the healing power of Jesus Christ to bear in the life of this man who obviously loved His Lord. "If this be possible, Lord, make it so. Giving You all the glory. Amen."

I looked up and his eyes were open. Stanley saw the people surrounding his bed, and the look on his face began to change. He began to smile, and his eyes were filled with life. In a deep, firm voice he said, "Now we must do what we can. Even though we have asked God for His blessing and His help, we must also do whatever we can to try to heal my body and to deal with this tumor. Let us proceed."

A man of faith was speaking to me. I stepped toward Stanley, reached out, and took his hand. As I did, I held on to the question of Why? Why was it necessary for this young man to go through this? Why, when he had already faced death once before? Why, when he had already lost his left leg? Why did he have to face death again?

I gripped his hand firmly. "Stanley, we must become positive and optimistic, and proceed with the surgery, doing what we can." His eyes didn't stop looking into mine. "I have noticed your hands, Dr. Cheatham. They are the hands of a surgeon. I know within my heart that God will work through you as you operate on my spine. Dr. Wesche tells me you are the first neurosurgeon ever to visit Tenwek Hospital. Therefore, I must believe that God brought you here at this time in order that my problem might be diagnosed and that you might operate on me and try to restore me to health."

As he spoke, his confidence just seemed to grow.

"I do not want to die, Dr. Cheatham. As a Christian, I know that I will not die. I may die in this earthly life, but Jesus has said that I, Stanley Cheborge, will never die. That is the promise given to me as a Christian, and that is the promise I believe. I may not survive the sickness in my body, but I will not die. No, I will not die."

Stanley's words accompanied me through the door of his room. But somewhere down the hallway, they were drowned out by the shout of that evening's demands. There was still a long line of patients waiting to see a surgeon. So many sick patients, and just a handful of doctors and nurses to care for them. And somewhere in the rush and hurry of my second day at Tenwek, Stanley Cheborge slipped from my consciousness.

I didn't stop working until after 10:00 p.m. It was dark when I walked back to our family's cramped, one-room guest quarters. By now I was very hungry. As Michael and I ate the dinner Sylvia had kept warm, around a small table, I saw four, tired faces. But there was the shared feeling that we had spent the day as the Lord would have us serving people in great need.

After about thirty minutes, I rolled my thoughts and my tired body into bed. I was so far from home and very preoccupied by the future facing one young Kipsigis man, and what it posed for my first neurosurgical operation at Tenwek. I found myself looking up at the ceiling wondering which challenge was greater. I would have to do the surgery using only spinal anesthesia since nothing else was available. This was something I was not used to doing. There was no anesthesiologist, no specialist to monitor Stanley while I operated. Inside I felt uneasy and a little bit frightened.

I opened my Bible to the words I needed to hear at that moment: "Yea, though I walk through the valley of the shadow of death, I will fear no evil for thou art with me." I suspected Stanley Cheborge might be contemplating the same words.

Soft, classical music from stereo headphones filled my head as I lay on the bed exhausted. Sleep was very close. I said a prayer of thanks to God for bringing our family safely to this place, and then I asked God to bless Stanley and all the other patients who waited for tomorrow to come. In the whisper of a moment I fell asleep.

The next morning as the sun rose on Kenya, I heard the singing of a thousand birds. I parted the drapes and peered out toward the hillside across the river. I could see people already making their way along the winding, dirt road toward the hospital. What other illnesses were coming to Tenwek? Which of these people would soon be looking to me to help them live?

I could see the first streams of sunlight coming over the hilltops and shining into the valley below as a heavy blanket of ground fog floated over the lush, green landscape. The river, twisting and muddy, became a dull roar in my ears as it spilled over the falls below the mission compound. The rhythmic chugging of the diesel generator, which supplied electricity for the hospital, continued without end.

Lord, let your hand be on mine as I operate on Stanley this morning.

These words were as real as the cup of coffee I held in my hands, hands that could make a difference in a young man's life, hands of a physician who knew the human body was very, very fragile.

What was surgery like that day? Why is it still so vivid in my mind? I can take you back to the hour and the moment, so you can experience it with me.

That morning I walked up the hill with Michael, my twenty-three-year-old-son, carrying the small black bags of special neurosurgical instruments we would need for the operation. Not yet a doctor, my son was already following me. He had always followed me, like a small shadow, almost from the time he had learned to walk. Now he was walking in my footsteps, following in my profession. I didn't mind this kind of company. In fact, I cherished it.

We went to Stanley's room. He was awake, smiling, unflinching.

"Good morning, my friend," I said as we entered the small room. "Did you sleep well?"

"Ah yes, yes, Dr. Cheatham, I have slept well. This morning I woke up early. And I have been praying for you, and for the success of my operation. For the Lord to heal my body."

If you could look around the room, you would see Annah standing near Stanley's bed and two of Stanley's brothers reclining on the other bed. As Stanley and I talked, I learned they had kept a vigil throughout the night. In the morning light, their faces were etched with doubt. Tired and subdued, they appeared to share none of the optimism of the one-legged man in the bed who smiled and talked confidently, even though he suspected his spine harbored cancer.

This was the prelude. After conducting some early rounds with Dr. Wesche, Michael and I walked with him to the operating theater. Just then Stanley was wheeled into the room. I could tell from his relaxed face that the pre-operative medications were taking hold. Still he remained very much awake.

"Dr. Cheatham, Dr. Wesche!" he said, as the gurney rolled in front of us. "Are you now ready? Are you prepared to do this thing, to operate on my spine?"

"Yes," we said. The final preparations were made. "Sister Kneubuhler is going to assist us as the scrub nurse. She is now getting ready the special instruments I brought from America. And Dr. Graber is going to come and monitor your blood pressure and pulse during surgery.

"You will be in good hands this morning."

"Of that I am assured," he responded, "because I have placed my life, not only in your hands, but in the Lord's."

While we chatted, Marty Graber must have been racing. The operation on Stanley meant everything to him. Yet I knew Marty's schedule was already bursting. Every day at Tenwek Hospital was a marathon for Marty, treating sick children in the tuberculosis ward. And always there was Ann, his wife, dressed in her white nurse's uniform and starched cap; she worked at his side as he moved from patient to patient.

Marty constantly faced outpatient emergencies. Because he had eleven years of experience in emergency medicine and had worked in the tuberculosis ward at Tenwek, Marty was called upon by the national staff to respond to the unexpected. All of these daily crises needed Marty's attention, his time, his physical and mental reserve. And now, in the rush of this ongoing barrage, he had chosen to come to the side of his close friend, who was facing the growing reality of cancer.

It was time to begin. "Stanley, are you ready?"

"I am ready," he answered in a soft, deep voice.

We turned Stanley over on his left side. Next, his lower back was prepped with the iodine solution from a bottle I had brought from California. I inserted the tip of the four-inch long spinal needle through the skin and ligaments of his lower back, one centimeter at a time, until it entered the spinal fluid sac. After aspirating a small amount of crystal clear cerebrospinal fluid, I slowly injected a solution of glucose and Pontocaine. At that moment I thought of Dr. Clark Wescoe, my medical school dean back in Kansas. He had become chairman of the board of the pharmaceutical company that made Pontocaine. In my mind's eye I could see him speaking. "If you attend my medical school, Mel, I will see to it that you become a real doctor—someone well rounded and capable." How could I have remembered his words at that moment, unless I believed they might have been true?

I withdrew the needle swiftly and Stanley was quickly turned onto his back. Within a few minutes he experienced a complete loss of feeling from his toes to his lower rib cage. All this time, Marty Graber kept a close watch on Stanley's blood pressure and pulse rate. As anticipated, the spinal anesthetic caused his blood pressure to fall. Marty increased the IV fluid rate and injected Ephedrin, a vasopressor drug, to raise Stanley's blood pressure and keep him from going into shock.

The staff rolled Stanley over onto the operating table where he would lie in a prone position. Steven Mabutu, the head surgical technician, placed blanket rolls under Stanley's hips and shoulders to elevate them and free his abdomen so he could breathe comfortably. Next, Steven scrubbed Stanley's back, and Denise Kneubuhler, an orthopedic surgical nurse from Indiana, covered his entire body with sterile surgical drapes. Only Stanley's lower spine was exposed.

Everything was almost ready. Denise had carefully laid out the surgical instruments on the sterile Mayo stand to my right.

Dr. Wesche and I had scrubbed and gowned and were standing opposite each other at the sterile draped operating table. Marty stood to my left, beyond the sterile field, where he could monitor Stanley's vital signs and administer IV fluids, medications, and blood.

The final task of preparing for surgery fell to Dr. Wesche. "Let us pray before we begin," he said.

"Lord, we ask for your blessing on Stanley. We ask you to guide each of us in the important task now before us. And we pray, dear Lord, that we will be your servants this morning as we operate on our friend and brother, Stanley. In the name of Jesus Christ, we pray. Amen."

Neurosurgery on the spine is always delicate. That morning there were added pressures. I had to work with a limited number of surgical instruments. This meant having to make some important compromises and having to improvise with those few available instruments. In addition to the challenges of what we might find inside Stanley's back, I felt another pressure. Stanley was one of the most respected and admired men in the entire Kipsigis tribe. As his relatives and friends waited outside in silence, I knew the outcome of this crucial operation weighed heavily on them.

So this was it—my first neurosurgery performed in an unfamiliar setting. Under less than ideal conditions. On a patient who probably had a tumor of the spine, that was almost certainly malignant. A condition that would make medical solutions impossible. On the morning of June 18, 1986, all of these concerns brought me to one simple, humbling realization: A young man who was greatly loved by his family, his friends, the staff of Tenwek, and a multitude of acquaintances—a man with a burning desire to live—now lay in front of me with the rest of his life in question. And he believed unswervingly that God would use me to heal him.

It was time. I have three pictures of what happened in the next three hours. They are snapshots that have been developed in my memory. And after the briefest moment spent remembering what it was like, the still figures in the picture come to life, the scene begins to move, and I am there. Again.

The first picture is Stanley's arm. I can see it on my left, beyond the sterile drapes, resting on the extended armboard. I can see the intravenous line carrying glucose solution and medications during the initial part of the operation. And I can see the same line carrying the blood that Marty would feverishly pump later on.

As I remember cutting into Stanley's lower back, a second picture emerges. It is everything I had seen in the X-rays. Except this time the intruding shape isn't confined to the X-ray film. It is no longer a suspected abnormality. The moment of truth is at hand. I can see it now. It is a tumor. I've seen enough tumors. I know what it is. It is cancer.

Bob Wesche saw it too. His eyes were filled with disappointment, a sadness we both shared. Ironically, the one person who slept soundly through this painful awareness was Stanley. With his brain numbed by the effects of sedation, he slept quietly. But I knew what real physical pain awaited him when he woke up.

The tumor, the picture of it frozen in my mind that morning, stared back at me. With a surgical instrument I touched its grayish-purple surface. Immediately there was brisk bleeding. I tried to remove pieces of it. But each time I looked, I saw more. My picture of this monstrous growth, buried deep in Stanley's lower back, grows dim when I see Marty Graber starting a blood transfusion to keep up with the blood Stanley was losing. Marty is shaking his head, and not saying a word. The cheerful man who had welcomed me to Tenwek two days before and already seemed like an old friend did not have words to express the disbelief or the quiet, unmistakable hurt I could see in his eyes.

The bleeding slowed. Soon it was under control. Yet the tumor remained. Bob Wesche and I had only one choice—to close the gaping operative wound. Successful surgery often brings on casual conversation while the patient is sewn up. But this morning we exchanged no more than a handful of words. I knew there was little we could do. And I still didn't now how prepared Stanley was to pursue the things he cared about passionately once he heard the bad news.

I already knew that Stanley's life had been showered with friendship, admiration, and love. Yet, one thing in life had seemed to have deserted him. Where was fairness? When cancer began eating away his future when he was just fifteen years old and caused him to lose his left leg, what happened to fairness? Why now, ten years and another lifetime later, did he have to face again the prospect of more suffering and a new threat of dying?

I stood over Stanley's motionless body, and I wondered. I remembered my childhood friend, Bobby, and the gunshot wound that ended his life. He was just five. And then, Ed Wright, who died in the prime of his life. Dr. Williamson, too, had died young—at age fifty-one. He had tried so hard to serve those who would not otherwise be served. He had cared for others more than himself, and it had cost him his life. If death is unfair, then it is also terribly perplexing and cruel. It had taken my three friends without thinking. Why did cancer have to take Stanley? Why, when he had so much life to live?

There was no time to answer these questions. I had only a few minutes to finish closing the operative wound before I moved on to the next patient who needed a surgeon.

When I think of that first neurosurgery, and feelings of relief mix with sadness, I see another picture. It doesn't reveal the intense medical preparation of the first scene or the sharp reality of the second. It is a picture of Stanley regaining consciousness as the sedation of surgery wears away. It shows a physician waking up to the fact that the time with Stanley was not over. In fact, perhaps it was just beginning.

For reasons I still do not understand, my picture of Stanley Cheborge grew. It enlarged beyond the temporary borders of my own expectations. Along with this picture, pasted like a snapshot in the scrapbook of my memory, is a caption, an accompanying explanation of who he was, and what he already meant to me.

I was beginning to see that Stanley was actually two people. First, there was Stanley the individual, my patient, who was quickly becoming my friend. But he was also someone else. Already I could see he was unique among his tribe. He was the booming, articulate voice that gave words and meaning to this quiet land of the Kipsigis. He spoke a language I could understand. At the same time he had an infectious, personal warmth that needed no words. He was a story filled with humor and a self-revealing nature that ignited my curiosity and caused me to say, "Tell me more." For me his extraordinary personality made Kenya come alive.

More than anything else though, Stanley was a living passport into the Third World for me. His candor, charisma, and faith seemed to give me a window through which I was able to see for the first time a culture I knew nothing about. Because of Stanley Cheborge, I began to understand better the physical and spiritual needs of others.

I remember how, following surgery, his eyes cracked open, adjusting to the light. When he was awake and alert enough to hear, I told him the news. "We got some of the tumor, Stanley, but not all." I can see his family, standing in the hallway, bracing for the announcement. Yet, Stanley remained calm. His bright, positive response to this harsh news puzzled me. And for those next few moments, and over the next few days, the faith and hope I saw in him forced me to ask again: Who is this Stanley Cheborge?

I began to have partial answers to that question, but not before waking up to the realities of working in an understaffed mission hospital.

The night following Stanley's surgery was my first time to be "on call" at Tenwek. Bob and Dora Wesche planned to leave at 7:00 a.m. the next morning to be away for three weeks. Carlos Somoza, the other surgeon, would not return from his vacation until the next evening. For the next twenty-four hours, I would be Tenwek's only surgeon.

At 2:00 a.m. my worst fears became reality. Michael and I were called to the outpatient area to see a small eight-year-old boy with a greatly distended abdomen. He was writhing with pain. With the help of X-rays, I diagnosed a bowel obstruction.

"Oh no!" I said to Michael. "He has to be operated on or he'll die. I don't look forward to doing such an operation in the middle of the night without an anesthesiologist or, at least, some help!"

Reluctantly I called Bob Wesche. "I know it's late, Bob. I know you and Dora will be driving seven hours to Nairobi in just a few hours. But Bob, I need your help in surgery. Now!"

Bob Wesche came over immediately. In the middle of the night, we did the surgery. We used Ketalar, a drug that makes the patient unconscious while he "sleeps" with his eyes fully open. This boy stared at Bob and me, totally unaware of what was going on in the room, while we removed about one foot of his lower intestine. At daybreak we finished the operation. The child was awake and stable. Bob left for Nairobi, and I walked up to Stanley's room and went in.

"How's my patient this morning?" I inquired.

"I am well," he said. "But you must be very tired. They told me of your long night in the operating theater. Please sit down and rest as we speak."

Stanley placed more importance on the state of my health and the extent of my fatigue than upon his own condition. That's why I had to insist that I inspect his operative wound and check his strength and sensation. Finally he realized he needed a doctor more than I did.

"I have little pain," he said. "But the Lord has blessed me with a good night's rest, and I know He is healing my body."

"You amaze me, my friend," I said. "You are sitting up in bed as if you had not had surgery yesterday. I have heard so much about you and how you came to know the Lord. Is it possible that you might tell me your life story?"

"Yes, if you have the time to listen, I will be very happy to tell you."

I was eager to learn more about this young man, and that afternoon, after church services, I made sure we had time to talk. This time I returned with company, my daughter, Elizabeth.

"Oh Elizabeth, it is my great pleasure to meet you," said Stanley, as he held out his long arm and then squeezed her soft, delicate hand in his strong grip. "I have met Michael and Robert, but now I am able to meet you."

"Stanley, Elizabeth plans to become a writer. If you tell us about your life, perhaps we can write your story someday so others can know you."

"Yes, of course, please sit down. I will tell you the story.

"I am of the Kipsigis tribe, born in a village called Lelaitich. It is located to the south, near the border frontier shared with the Maasai tribe. From my home it is possible to see far into the distance across the plains of the Maasai Mara. There my mother gave birth to me, in a round, mud-walled hut with a cone-shaped

Michael, Robert and Elizabeth on safari in 1986

Peaceful young lion

The Maasai village where the Cheathams had their first glimpse into African life and culture

Elephants—a majestic and common sight on the African plain

Mel and Sylvia on a game run during their first trip to the land they would grow to love

Pat Chaney helps a young Kenyan pound manioc (an African plant similar to spinach and a high-protein item in the Kenyans' diet).

Stanley in Tenwek's bustling courtyard

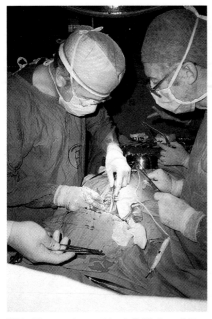 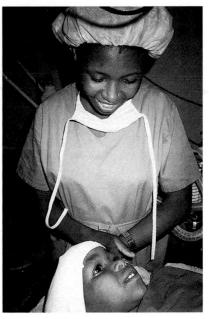

"We Treat—Jesus Heals" Mel and Dr. Ernie Steury at work

One of the "gracious Kenyan nurses" assists a brain tumor patient in recovery.

Families are close at Tenwek. Here, a young patient is visited by a relative.

Medical supplies that comprised many of the eighteen pieces of luggage for the Cheathams' first trip to Tenwek

Touch-down at Tenwek!

The Cheathams are greeted by a host of Nationals upon arrival at Bomet Airstrip.

Dr. Bob Wesche dressed to serve.

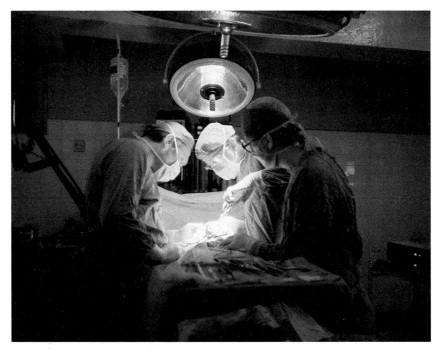

Mel and Bob Wesche practicing their profession

A cheerful Nora Caffrey prepares the surgical instruments.

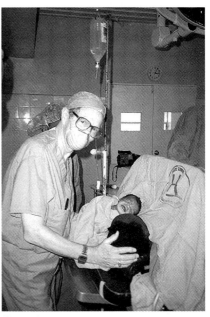

One of many successful ceserean deliveries

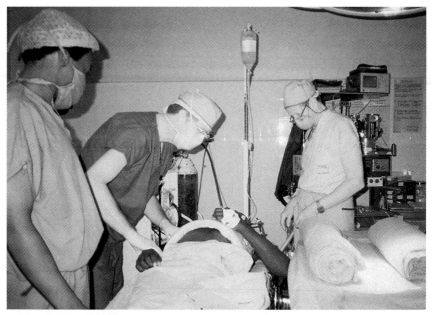

Stanley being moved to the surgical table just before his operation

Elizabeth with Stanley as he sits on his thin mattress on the ground

Stanley and friends at graduation

Stanley displays his famous "toothy grin" in front of an African hut.

Stanley engaged in his favorite
pursuit—teaching the Word of God

Stanley in his "Sunday best"

Pat Chaney holding Stanley's daughter, Grace Cherotich Cheborge

Recovering brain tumor patient

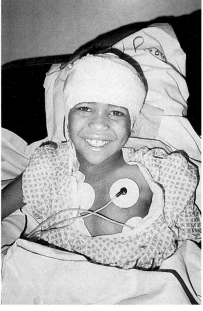

Tenwek's first brain tumor patient is all smiles after a successful operation.

Dr. Nellie Mac, "Uncle" Charlie Snyder, and Sylvia

Kenyan surgical technicians receive instruction from Nora Caffrey.

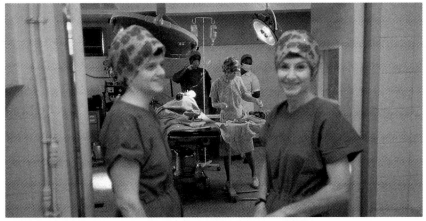

Judy Streamer and Sylvia in Tenwek's scrub room

(From left) Dr. Susie Cheatham, Dr. Michael Cheatham, Dr. Mel and Sylvia Cheatham, Steven Mabutu, Dr. Bill and B.J. Martin

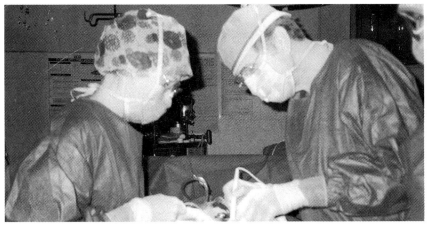

Sylvia often proved a valuable assistant to Mel in the operating room.

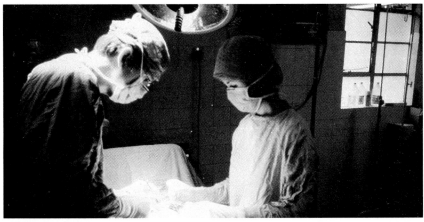

Elizabeth assisting her father in surgery

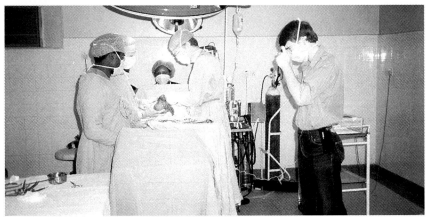

Robert photographing an operation.

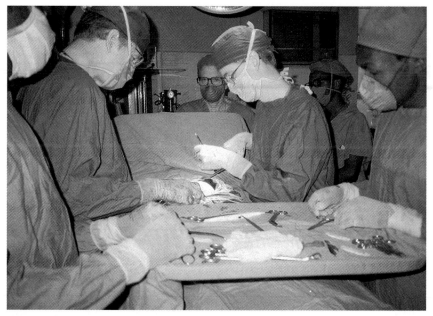

Father and son (Mel and Michael) operating together

The Cheatham family (from left): Michael, Elizabeth, Robert, Sylvia and Mel

A once-paralyzed, fully recovered Lilly Tesot and her family

Mel stands beside a much-needed Land Rover provided by World Medical Mission.

roof of tightly thatched grass. I do not know exactly when this was, but I believe it was in 1959."

The Kipsigis boy I had imagined as I was on the plane the first time I departed from Kenya, and his culture that I was sure I would never know, was now sitting in front of me. I could tell he was prepared to tell me everything.

"I was born as the next to last of twelve children. Fate later placed me in the position of youngest in our family. This occurred because of the death of my younger brother. You do not know, but as the youngest, I am charged with the responsibility of caring for my parents in their old age. This I am happy to do, because our tribal culture says it is something I *must* do. I am happy to do this, because I love my mother and my father, even as they love me.

"You see," he continued, "I was not sure who my mother was until I was about four. This was because there were so many small children in the village, and the mothers were too busy with their work to care individually for each child. From an early age, it was necessary for us to take care of ourselves.

"But even as a very small child, I knew who my father was. I feared him. I respected him. I loved him dearly as my father. Many times while growing up I found myself in danger. My father would suddenly appear, and he would protect me. At other times, I faced danger and he was not there. But I always followed the course I knew my father would take, and my safety was assured. From an early age, I knew that I must follow closely in my father's footsteps, and doing so gave me great pleasure."

"I have seen where the Maasai live," I said. "It was when our family came to Kenya for the first time several years ago." I thought of the children we had met, their faces covered with flies, and all the children and adults whose names I didn't know. Everything I knew about their history and way of life I could fit on a postcard, and still have room for a postscript.

"Like the Maasai, the huts in our village have not changed in many, many years," Stanley said. And I realized that Elizabeth and I were not hearing just one man's story. We were learning the history of an entire culture.

"In my mother's hut, where life came to me, things were very primitive. The hut had a mud floor, and the chickens nested inside at night. Into this simple way of life I was born."

Then Stanley paused and made sure we were listening. "Do you know, Elizabeth, that the Bible tells me my Savior, Jesus Christ, was born in similar surroundings? I feel that I have been privileged to be born and to live simply as it was with Jesus.

"You probably wonder where a Kipsigis would get a name like Stanley, right?"

"You must have a story for that," Elizabeth said. And, of course, he did. It was a story that showed both of us how strikingly removed Stanley's world was from our's.

"*Kiprotich* was the name given to me at birth. It is the same name given to all newborn Kipsigis boys born at a certain time of day. Before I was called Stanley, I was known by another name, Gibson. How I received this name will tell you more about Kipsigis than the name itself.

"Our tribal tradition believes that the spirit of life is passed on from one family member to another. When a family member dies, the body is buried so that it will not be eaten by a wild animal. This is done to enable the spirit within the person to be resurrected within the body of a new member of the family.

"This is what happens: The women in the family gather around the infant and watch closely for the 'sneeze.' They ask the baby, again and again, if he or she is the departed grandfather, uncle, brother or other relative. There can be long waiting. But eventually the baby responds to the name of a dead relative. The baby sneezes and that signals the spirit of the dead relative who has entered the baby. That is the way life continues. I sneezed after my mother mentioned the name 'Gibson,' so that became my first name."

I was captivated by Stanley's story. For the first time I could glimpse inside another culture. Because Stanley didn't seem to want to stop, I settled myself more firmly on the wooden stool and forgot about my watch.

"The name Stanley came later. It was of my choosing. It is not a common name among the Kipsigis. It was the name of the famous explorer, H. M. Stanley, who came to Africa years ago in search of Dr. David Livingstone."

"So that's why you chose Stanley?" I asked.

"I chose it because it had been the name of someone great, a person who was fearless and famous. This is how I imagined myself early in my life, the way I was before . . ."

Although I had yet to hear the whole story, I knew where he was going. I just had no idea of the stark conditions, the raw, everyday obstacles he woke up to every morning.

"Do you know what it is like to get up before the sun each day, Elizabeth? From the time I was six, I helped herd our family's goats and cattle. I did this all day long.

"I would look after as many as twenty animals at a time, and try not to lose any or let them wander into fields where crops were growing."

"Did you do this all by yourself?" Elizabeth asked.

"Yes, many times. I was alone with them in the day, and before darkness I had to drive them back to a sheltered area where the wild animals could not eat them or the Maasai come and steal them."

I imagined myself looking out on the silent Kansas plains of my childhood. I never journeyed more than a shout from the back door of our home. At age six, Stanley Cheborge was already carrying adult responsibilities. At an age when I was reading about cowboys fighting enemies to protect animals and land, he was doing all of this just to survive. It meant he had to sleep with half an eye open at night to spot all kinds of preditors who coveted his flock—not only the two-legged animal with a spear, but the four-legged beast with a savage appetite as well.

"When it got warm, there would be another danger— snakes. I had to learn from older boys how to avoid the paths and areas where snakes would hide and then come out to look for food. I learned to look in trees. That's where cobras like to rest. In the tall grass were black mambas and puff adders. Their bite is quick and deadly."

"How did you protect yourself?" Elizabeth asked.

"Against poisonous snakes, the best weapon is knowing where not to walk at night." I wondered but didn't ask Stanley if he had learned this lesson the hard way.

"As a herder I carried a rungut. That is a club two feet long, made from a tree limb. I used a panga knife and a bow and arrows."

Stanley described how the soles of his feet grew to be thick and numb, as he covered miles of brush, rock, and sand. He mentioned, when he was five, how his father told him that he would need to help care for the family calves. And Stanley did so without question. As a Kipsigis, one never disobeys his father. And as one of twelve children, Stanley learned early that he was responsible for himself. There were no alternatives.

This explained the calluses on his feet. And I thought I was beginning to understand how Stanley gained his great spirit and determination. However, his childhood seemed no more exceptional than thousands of Kipsigis boys who obeyed their fathers and then walked barefoot into a hungry, unforgiving world. Still, this young man was unusual. His body was taller. His voice was deeper. His personality was the whisper-like manner of most other Kipsigis men pulled inside-out. It revealed a person who engaged me with warmth, humor and confidence, and he refused to take credit for any of it.

"I cannot count how many days I spent alone in the bush country near my home. That is where I thought to myself. That is when I dreamed."

"What did you dream about?" Elizabeth asked.

"During those times of solitude in the bush, I dreamt how I would build my future wealth and greatness. I was so restless. I was ambitious. I felt this aggressive spirit growing inside me. But the thing I wished most for was to be powerful. I did not want to be a lonely goat herder the rest of my life.

"By the time I was fourteen, I could feel my urge for power growing. And I knew I would not have to wait long until the moment that would change me and allow me to achieve my dream."

Stanley stared up at the ceiling as if he knew something loomed beyond this turn in his story. What did he see? Why was he suddenly so reflective, after he had been an endless stream of information?

"Stanley, I want to hear more," I said. My words seemed to pull him away from a long-ago time and back to the present moment.

"There is more to my story, and I will tell it to you," he said. He looked toward Elizabeth, then back to me. "Dr. Cheatham, the rest I will tell you another time." As he spoke, I sensed that the rest of the story would be only for me to hear. I was willing to wait.

I got up from the stool with two things equally certain in my mind. First, I would quickly be buried under the needs of some very sick patients. And second, one of them had begun to crack open his life, allowing me to see into a new and different world in which I was no longer just a visitor.

SIX

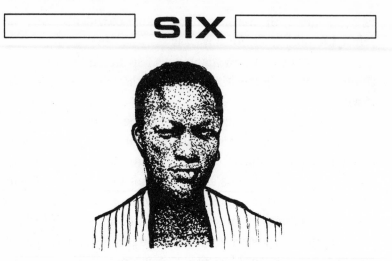

Dr. David Stevens, the medical director at Tenwek Hospital, stood in the doorway of the operating theater as I finished another operation.

"Mel, how is your work coming?"

"Fine, Dave," I responded.

"I've just been over in the outpatient area and they've just brought in a young man who can't move anything with much strength, except his shoulders. I think he may have a broken neck. We're getting X-rays," David said. "Do you have time to look at him?" I could sense some urgency and concern in Dave's voice. "I'm afraid if his neck is broken, the bones may slip further and sever his spinal cord, rendering him permanently paralyzed."

I certainly understood Dave's concern and quickly finished writing my orders on my current patient's chart. Then immediately I went with Dave to the X-ray department. "Sorry I haven't had any time with you since your arrival at Tenwek," he said, "but my administrative work has kept me tied up almost full-time. This afternoon I finally decided I'd had enough paper work, reports, and meetings, so I came over to help with the outpatient load."

Solomon, the X-ray technician, handed me the picture, and I took it into the small doctor's office next door and placed it up on the lighted view-box where David and I could study it. The neck was indeed broken. The fifth cervical vertebra was displaced forward onto the sixth cervical vertebra, and the space for the spinal cord was markedly narrowed. This meant that with the slightest movement, additional irreparable damage to the spinal cord could occur. The grave risk of such permanent inability to move or experience any sensation or feeling from the neck and shoulders downward is always frightening. We needed to quickly stabilize the fractured spine.

"Where is the patient?" I asked David. He took me to the outpatient treatment room where I found the young nineteen-year-old man lying on his back on a gurney cart. Two of his brothers had carried him the several miles from his home to Tenwek.

Someone in the group explained, "He fell from the back of a matatu when it hit a bump."

As I examined the patient, I noted marked weakness in his lower extremities and to a degree his upper. The pattern of weakness and loss of sensation confirmed his spinal cord injury. Still, he was not completely paralyzed. There was some hope.

I told Michael, "He needs to be placed in a Halo brace so that we can re-align his spinal vertebra and hold them in a safe position until he can be fused."

A Halo brace gets its name from a round rim that encircles the patient's head. Metal pins screwed in tightly against the skull hold it in place. The halo is then connected by rods, nuts, and bolts to a firm-fitting, sheepskin-lined body jacket so the entire mechanism keeps the neck spine immobile. At $2,400 apiece, such a brace would have been out of the question for this young man. Ordinarily, the chances of finding a Halo brace at Tenwek Hospital were about as great as discovering an artificial heart transplant operation in progress there. Fortunately, we had brought with us to Tenwek five used Halo braces that had been washed and sanitized after being used by patients in America so they could be used again.

My son Bob arrived shortly from his post in the hospital central supply carrying a duffel bag containing the vests. Inspecting each one, I chose the one that best fit the patient. Then I showed Dr. Wesche how to apply the brace to the young man so the spinal vertebra in his neck were aligned correctly. Some staff members and a few patients, who waited nearby, were looking on, and I could tell the procedure made a great impression on them. This was a treatment they could clearly see, and it had real meaning for them.

Some hours later, a man somewhat older than the first Halo brace patient, was brought in. He had been in a fight and also had a broken neck. But his condition was much worse. He was totally paralyzed below his upper arms. I could see that he was going to stay that way. Still, we placed him in one of the Halo braces. The treatment couldn't restore his sense of feeling or his ability to move, but the brace would make caring for him easier.

Who would think two Halo braces would be needed within the span of a few hours at a remote mission hospital that had never before had such a brace on hand? I chuckled to myself, wondering if I should bring out a third brace for the next emergency that came in the door.

A doctor, whether he or she is in the emergency room of a modern U.S. medical center or in a Third World mission station like Tenwek Hospital, must be prepared for anything, including the most remarkable coincidences. Within twenty-four hours, I was standing again in the treatment room. This time I was examining a seventy-year-old Kipsigis woman who had been kicked in the head by a cow. She also had a broken neck. Luckily she was not paralyzed, but chances are she would have been if we'd been unable to put her in the one thing she needed at that moment: a Halo brace.

The next morning I saw her on the hospital compound, and she was walking! There was a certain dignity about her you would have to have seen to believe. She was proud of her brace, and so aware of it that she had draped her colorful Kitanga sheet over the top of the steel halo ring around her head. The bright red, green, and yellow cloth flowed down her back. The brace gave her real stature and seemed to set her apart from the other members of her tribe. Something I had packed in a suitcase—a piece of medical equipment I might have taken for granted in the U.S.—had found a perfect fit in the Third World.

All this went on while Stanley rested in his room and dealt with the reality of cancer. I had brought more than five Halo braces, however. I had brought with me a desire to belong to Tenwek Hospital and a desire to know the Kipsigis. The meeting with Stanley, his operation, and his interest in me had touched me deeply. Any more time I had with him would be limited to brief visits in his room. That was the hurry-up reality of Tenwek. People came constantly through the door—needing surgery, needing medication, needing to give birth to babies. They needed help, not in a little while, but immediately. All this left me precious little time to stop and get to know a patient, including the one person who had broken through the Kipsigis language barrier and allowed me to learn something of this land and its people.

By the third or fourth day at Tenwek there was a pattern and a rhythm and flow of what to expect. After breakfast, I showered, then climbed into a green scrub suit and prepared for rounds. I started with the women. If you had walked with me on these early-morning visits, you would have seen how a hospital in the Third World was equipped to care for its patients. You would see them sitting on the grass outside the concrete block buildings, enjoying the sun and morning air. The women would look at me, but wouldn't say anything. Some might smile, then quickly turn their faces away in shyness. Why were they in the hospital? Many were pregnant. Some were waiting to give birth, others required C-sections, and some were still bleeding after miscarriages. It was strange to see patients sitting on the lawn, until I began to discover the clean air and feel the warm sun myself.

I would go inside and walk down the long hallways of smooth cement, seeing and smelling the world I greeted each morning. The rooms were large enough to hold twenty narrow beds, especially when placed side-by-side in two long rows. In the entrance way, a Kipsigis woman might be pouring buckets of water on the floor, then using what looked like a large windshield wiper blade made of wood to push the water along. Without mops, industrial strength cleaners, and electric-buff waxers, the hospital relied on cold water to take care of dirt and to wash away the mud tracked in by hundreds of bare feet.

Every bed was filled, some not with just one patient, but two. Often the head of one person and the feet of another rested on the same pillow. If you stopped for a moment, you would notice something else. Silence. Though there were thirty patients in one room, there was no chatter and no laughter. It was eerie, a reminder that the Kipsigis lived within themselves. As I walked with the interpreter from bed to bed, I could feel the eyes of every patient watching me.

Walk from bed to bed and you would see what made these people sick: A young mother has had a tubal ligation; barely in her thirties, she has already given birth to nine babies and miscarried several others. Another woman, somewhat older, has a large tumor on her forehead. Still another, her abdomen bloated and her eyes yellow with jaundice, has hepatitis. Another woman has a huge sore on her left hip. It was probably caused by a small puncture wound which then became severely infected, forming a deep abscess. The entire area gapes open, exposing layers of red muscle. Whitish hip bone shines in its depths. The smell of pus and dead muscle is overpowering.

Most of these patients could leave the hospital in two or three days. Some would need to remain longer. Some knew they might never leave. All waited patiently. All waited in complete silence.

Come with me to the pediatrics ward. It is a zoo. Children crying. Children coughing. One is squirming away from a nurse's needle. Another is trying to get out of bed. These are very sick kids—kids with diarrhea, measles, and encephalitis. Some have congenital problems. One child has a huge tumor growing out of the side of his face. The nurses made a gauze cap to fit over it. Still the other kids teased him.

In the midst of this large group of sick children, Dr. Dick Morse and Robyn Moore, a registered nurse, would examine one, then another, and another. Elizabeth and Robert took balloons along as toys. A child who had never seen a balloon filled with air before his eyes was a child enthralled. Unfortunately, balloons couldn't cure the illnesses these kids would wake up with each morning. They needed rest, and medicine, and someone to sit with them.

At Tenwek I saw an amazing reminder of what it is like for a child to be in the hospital, and what it means to be family. Every morning, without exception, when I walked into the children's ward, I saw mothers and fathers sitting on the beds with their kids. Many of them rarely left. When one Kipsigis becomes sick, the entire family goes with him or her to the hospital. I began to try to think of any families I knew back in California who would be willing to walk five, twenty, or fifty miles to the hospital, and then stay at the bedside of a sick relative until he or she was better. I couldn't come up with many names.

If we walked into the burn ward, you would see about a dozen children. And you would be able to smell their burns. This was one of the hardest sights to look at: a young child who had fallen into the fire of his family's hut, a fire kept burning twenty-four hours a day for cooking and warmth. I would inspect the child and determine when he or she would be ready for a skin graft. Because I wanted each girl and boy to be well, this delicate procedure could never come too soon. I was thankful for the four months I'd spent as a resident in plastic surgery. Because of that training, I was able to do skin grafts on those children at Tenwek, so many years later.

Our morning rounds would not be complete until we had walked through the male ward with more rows of sick, silent patients, sometimes two in a bed. A young man is recovering from a bowel obstruction. An older man has prostate cancer. I remember seeing a man who was missing part of his right ear. Someone had bitten it off in a fight, and then swallowed it. For a Kipsigis this was the ultimate humiliation and shame.

Biting off and swallowing an ear. Falling into a cooking fire as a child. Sitting on the hospital lawn as a patient. These things are what made Kenya a foreign country to me. I wanted to understand them, but how? How do you tackle the meaning of an entire culture in six weeks? Behind every silent patient, every disease, was a person, someone with a story and a life locked away from me in a language and a culture I did not know.

One morning, several days after Stanley's surgery, I had a few extra minutes. Michael and I decided to stop by Stanley's room.

"Dr. Cheatham! Michael! You have decided to pay me a visit." Stanley was lying on his side. Four days following spinal surgery, most people often feel severe pain. I couldn't understand the look on Stanley's face. He was smiling. And the smile wasn't pasted on. His joy was real.

"How are you feeling, my friend?" I asked.

"Very fine. Very good," he replied.

"Do you feel much pain in your back?" I asked.

"There is pain," he said. "Still, I know this is something I must accept for now, until the Lord brings healing to my body. Until then, I am prepared to wait and to accept that which I cannot change."

I checked Stanley's wound. It was healing well. I had been at Tenwek almost a week, and Stanley had yet to ask about the new artificial leg we had brought with us. I was anxious to get him on his feet to see if he could walk with it.

"What if Michael and I help you put on the new leg?" I asked him.

There was a look of optimism in his eyes, a look that said, "Once I get this new leg, once I stand and begin to walk, things will be all right."

While Stanley lay on his right side, Michael and I fastened the chocolate-brown artificial leg to his stump. He was all smiles. I now saw what had first been an awkward piece of luggage for what it really was: Stanley Cheborge's long-awaited hope to walk again. With delicate determination, Michael and I raised Stanley to a sitting position. Then we helped him stand and brought all his weight to bear on both legs. For a moment I saw Stanley Cheborge, confidently standing on two legs. "Come walk with me, Dr. Cheatham," he invited.

He took a couple of steps with the new limb, short, halting steps. Like a tire punctured by a sharp object, the smile on Stanley's face went flat. Something was wrong. He stopped, and I could see little beads of perspiration had formed on his brow.

"The pain is too great," he said.

Those five simple words extinguished the past ten years of hope. He backed up and sat down on the bed. Quickly we helped him lie down, then unfastened the leg. The spark of optimism that so often lit up his room was gone. A moment passed before he could regain his composure. Tears welled up in his eyes. Michael decided to leave quietly. Now it was just Stanley and me. After awhile, when the severity of the pain had diminished, Stanley said, "I want to tell you something. For the last ten years, ever since I lost my leg, I have been a man who is just learning to walk. It was no problem for me to cover many miles a day on one leg and a stick, then a crutch, and finally an artificial leg. It has been so many years since I ran, I sometimes forget who that person was who could stand and run and walk on two feet."

"Can you think back to that earlier time?" I asked the question gingerly, not wanting to re-open a chapter of his life that might have been too painful to recall.

"Dr. Cheatham, I have thought of what to tell you about myself. I can tell you are a man who cares about others, and who takes the time to listen. The story that I began to tell you and Elizabeth the other day, there is more. Most Americans, most visitors to our land, have never heard this story. Yet, I can tell it to you. By hearing my story you will see the things I used to live for."

"What kind of things?" I asked.

"Possessions and power. I knew these desires could never come true until the time of my passage into manhood. We say it 'Bendi Banda.' It means 'they are going on a journey with a special purpose.' And this is that journey.

"It was December, the hottest, driest time of the year in Kenya, the time the circumcision ceremony would be performed. I knew it would take four weeks, all beginning with that first ceremony. It started one evening. We were all together, all the young boys and their fathers. My father was there and all the elders of the tribe. There was singing into the night. All the men sang Kipsigis songs. They wanted us to be prepared, to know what to expect.

"'You must be brave,' they said, 'so that when the cut is made, you will not move, or cry out, or show any sign of pain, emotion, or fear. If you fail in this, you will be marked a coward, and not a man, for the remainder of your life.'

"I remember walking into the ceremonial hut with all the other boys. We were dressed in short goat and sheep skins and seated with our legs apart. Behind me stood my father. In the flickering fire light, with shadows on the wall, I could barely see him, even though he was as large as a giant to me. I was not ready for what happened next. My father put a long spear with the sharp point behind my neck, and I heard him say, 'This spear could save your life, or it could take your life.' Every father in the room said this because every one held a spear to his son's head!"

I did not have an index file in my own childhood experience to look up such a scene. It just didn't exist. And yet if I had been Stanley, I would have felt the same fear. The boy in him must have been frightened, while the man waited to emerge.

"Then I lifted my head and looked across the fire that burned in the center of the circle. I looked at the small doorway and the first light of dawn was coming into the hut. It was time for the next part of the ceremony to begin.

"That was left to an elder of the tribe. He walked forward and knelt down. The last thing I remember was the machete. In one swift, slicing blow, it came down on me. It was only slight at first. But soon my body was pulsating. I shook back and forth within my body but never once did I show how bad it hurt outside where others might see. In fact, I looked straight ahead. It was the greatest moment of my life. My pride was numb. My body was bleeding. I wanted it all to stop and, at the same time, to go on.

"But the ceremony was not finished. I saw the elder move from each person, each initiate, moving in a slow, dark circle with his knife. I could feel my heart racing. Blood was flowing freely from my body. I could feel it, but I looked straight ahead. I was now closer to the moment of greatness I had waited for all my life.

"Other elders came into view. They moved forward and applied moist grass and cow manure to the bleeding area. The mixture had been boiled and made into a poultice to slow the bleeding and ward off infection. At first it only made the pain worse, but then its warmth became soothing. By now it was very late. I was exhausted, like every boy in the room, from this night that was like no other. Finally, we were allowed to sleep.

"For the next two weeks, I did not see the sun. I had to remain inside the ceremonial hut. That is the custom. Only at night, only when I had to, was I allowed to be in the open air. When I left, I had to use a special stick and strike one side of the hut's low doorway, then the other side. And then I had to do the same coming back in.

"You may think it was impossible to stay in the hut and to be silent the entire time, for fourteen days. For me there was only one thing that was hard, and that was to mask the thrill in my head. 'I am going to be the most powerful Kipsigis in my tribe. I will gain wealth and land and cattle and power and everywhere people will know the name, Stanley Cheborge!'

"The third week was the greatest test. Without warning, along with the others, I was taken outside the hut and led to the Mengit River, to the place just before it flows into the great Mara River. There the water was deeper and wider. And I knew the next part of my passage to manhood waited.

"I knew my father and the other men of the tribe had been busy at the river. I did not know that in the middle of the river they had built a mound of sticks and the branches of stinging nettles before constructing a dam that had raised the muddy water level to six feet. I did not know that a thorny, prickly obstacle lay ahead, lining each side of the pathway through the water.

"We arrived at the river's edge near dusk. We walked in silence. We were naked and barefoot, and we could feel the dusty, parched soil. By the time we reached the water, each boy was covered with chalky dust. Dressed in nothing but long shadows, we must have looked eerie, all standing there, ready to meet the darkness of the river. I felt a cool breeze blow against my sweaty body. And I waited.

"Then, suddenly, a fear ran up my back, and I knew why. A year before, in this same river, my younger brother, Kipketwol, the last born in the Cheborge family, had drowned. Even though he was younger than I, we had planned to walk together through this important rite. His body was not found for seven days. His death made me the youngest son, meaning I had been bestowed with the great responsibility of caring for my parents in the future. When old age overtook them, their needs, their well-being would now fall on me.

"Now, standing, shivering at the water's edge, I thought about dying. That's when an elder led me into the water. It was icy cold. Chill hit my toes and stopped me. Quickly, without thinking, I took a deep breath to stop the involuntary gasp that threatened to burst from my throat. My chest pounded. I felt as if it might explode with fear.

" 'I must go on,' I thought. With every step, every inch, the cold came up over me, meeting the heat from my body and making me tremble. I could not take my eyes off the trees and brush on the other shore. And then the pain! The stinging, searing feeling on my skin. Only now can I picture the sight, hidden below—millions of stinging nettles digging into my naked body. I could not let the pain show. I couldn't, even as I felt my head sink below the river's murky surface.

"It was like an underwater burial. Dark. Totally dark. I hungered to breathe. Just one breath! And then panic, as I saw my brother's body floating in that very place. In a few seconds, I was looking up. I could see sky and brush. As the water drained from my eyes, I saw the elders watching from the opposite shore. And I said to myself, 'Show no pain.'

"Now I could see the other boys in front of me. The backs of their legs and their shoulders and arms were covered with scratches and cuts. First my chest, then my stomach, and then my legs rose out of the water as I stepped to shore. First I stumbled, then my staggered steps became long strides, up the side of the river. Silently, inside myself, I shouted, 'I have made it! I have emerged from the river! I have triumphed!'

"Why was I so happy? I had to turn and repeat the passage back to the other side, for a total of four passes. But now the fear of the unknown was gone. I felt a smirk spread across my face. I felt myself approaching manhood. And after the fourth pass through the water, the procession of elders and boys emerged on shore. 'Hey-ya! Hey-ya! Hey-ya!' Then they all collapsed on the dusty ground. The whiteness of the chalk that had covered my body was now washed away. I was wearing new skin, the new skin of manhood etched with a hundred bleeding scratches and cuts from the stinging nettle bushes which stood hidden in the blackness of the water.

"I was coming to the end that led to my beginning. We stayed at the river's edge through the night. At the first rays of sun, we destroyed the structure of pain which had blistered our bodies. Then I was led to a narrow point in the river where the two banks were separated by only five feet. Across from where I stood, I could see a spear sticking out from the ground. It's deadly point was aimed directly at my heart.

"The elder standing next to it looked at me. His voice was clear and loud when he called out, 'Jump across the water onto the spear.'

"'No!' I said to myself. But the voice of manhood was louder. I knew I had to obey to prove I was brave. In one leap I threw myself into the air, toward the spear, toward death. In midair my body froze. Hands gripped my arms and my legs. They were the hands of my father on one side and the chief on the other. My life had been saved. In the powerful grip of my father's hands I experienced pain, but also the realization of his love and his pride and courage.

"I walked back to the ceremonial pool. I felt ten feet tall. And at the pool I saw the shape of a female body made of mud. I was told that represented a woman, unclean and unwelcome in this ceremony for men. I was given two sticks and told to strike the image. One stick I cast aside as tainted with uncleanness; the other stick I carried back to the ceremonial hut so that I could use it 'to strike any living woman should I encounter the same along the way.'

"The final night had come. With the others I put on long animal skins and sang ancient ceremonial songs. Through the night we built a small, symbolic hut called a 'Tomnet.' And when the morning came, we took it outside and burned it. Our time inside the hut was ended.

"In the new morning, I made the final pilgrimage to the Mara River to wash myself of the dirt and blood so that my new skin of manhood might be seen. With new animal skins to wear, including one to cover my head, I sat in contemplation about my mother and my home. Then, arriving at my mother's hut, a small girl, a woman, and an old man joined me as I prepared to enter. I entered through the gate and my mother performed the final ritual. She removed the animal skin from my head and replaced it with a crown.

"At that moment I knew I had achieved my goal. I was finally a man. The next morning, obeying her instructions, I returned to her hut where she removed my crown and then shaved my head with a sharp panga knife. I removed my long animal skins, dressed myself in regular clothes, and then stood as a man.

"Only one thing remained. Even though I was officially a man, I could not speak to females for one week. And not until my father gave his invitation could I enter my mother's hut or sleep inside it.

"Those days were the loneliest for me, Dr. Cheatham. I longed for one thing, and that was for the acceptance of my father. I deeply loved and respected him."

I tried to take in everything that this young man had told me, but that was barely possible. Outside his room the flurry of Tenwek Hospital raced by.

"I must go, Stanley," I said. "You have told me so much. But there is so much more I want to hear."

"You will, Dr. Cheatham. There will be another time."

I knew his story was not finished. Nor were my questions, such as where had his lust for wealth and power taken him? The fourteen-year-old initiate was not the same man as the one now looking at me with a contagious smile. He had already been saved once by his father and the tribal chief. What had kept Stanley from fulfilling his unquenchable desires? I didn't know how many more days Stanley would be at Tenwek. But I had to make time to hear the rest of his story. However, I knew the minute I stepped outside his room there would be another drama and another patient waiting for me.

I carried the images of Stanley's initiation with me as I made my way through the crowded schedule of surgeries. Like Stanley, standing on the edge of the river bank, I knew what was demanded of me every time I stepped into the operating theater—that was helping another patient and sometimes saving another life.

A twenty-two-year-old woman came in one afternoon complaining of sudden, severe abdominal pain. Marilyn Van Kuiken, a registered nurse, saw her initially in the outpatient area, and made a tentative diagnosis of a ruptured ectopic pregnancy. Marilyn had been a missionary nurse a long time before, and I knew few others who had the gift of her knowledge and experience.

We laid the woman on the examining table. I felt her abdomen, and it was tender. The pain had begun too suddenly for it to be caused by a ruptured appendix. Besides, the tenderness was over the left lower abdomen, not the right. I needed another physician to examine her with me. I knew Marty Graber was nearby. "Marty, do you have time to look at a patient?" He did, and a few moments later he inserted a long needle into the girl's abdomen and aspirated blood. This meant she probably had a ruptured ectopic pregnancy, where the fetus was developing in the fallopian tube next to the uterus, instead of in the uterus itself. If this were the case, she could easily bleed to death.

She was going into shock. I gave her a liter of IV fluid rapidly in order to raise her blood pressure and then some Ketalar. I opened her abdomen. It was filled with blood. She did have an ectopic pregnancy, but it had ruptured and was bleeding briskly into her abdominal cavity. I moved as quickly and as carefully as I could. I tied a suture around the site of the bleeding. Then, I placed sutures tightly around the arteries and veins to the enlarged fallopian tube in which the abnormal pregnancy had formed, and removed it. Finally, I evacuated all of the blood. The whole procedure took less than twenty minutes. She would live.

The surgeries continued non-stop, from mid-morning, after rounds and a break for a tea, milk, and sugar drink called "chai," until a one-hour lunch break, from 1:00 to 2:00 p.m. Then it was back into the operating theater for three to four more hours of surgeries. The patients came in the door, one after another, in no particular order. Often they shared only one common denominator: *urgent*. Dr. Somoza helped me remove a prostate gland from a seventy-year-old man. I repaired an umbilical hernia on a small child. Then we removed a cancerous breast that threatened a young woman's life.

I will never forget the little girl who was brought in with a leg that had been cut open. When I heard how, I almost couldn't believe it. She was suffering from congenital heart disease and malaria, but there was more. The greatest pain was in her tibia, one of the major bones in the lower leg, where pus had accumulated. The mother explained through the interpreter that the child's pain had become so great that the little girl took a machete knife and whacked open her own leg to let the pus pour out!

What I looked at was skin and bones. Under spinal anesthesia, I scraped out the bone cavity and washed out the pus, and then packed the long gaping wound open so it could drain. She stayed in the hospital for several weeks. I learned later that in two months she was walking again.

Children are not easy to forget. I can see their faces, and I remember their tears. I can still see a certain eighteen-year-old boy and recall how close he was to dying. He was a patient of Marty Graber's up in the TB ward. Bob Wesche was away on vacation. That left Carlos Somoza, a surgeon from Buenos Aires, and me to look after this boy who had pulmonary tuberculosis. The disease had already formed a large cavity in the upper lobe of his left lung. Worse yet he was hemorrhaging right in front of us; blood from the lung was coming out through his mouth. We had to act fast.

What we desperately needed was to call in an experienced chest surgeon, but that was impossible. Realizing that if anything was done we would have to do it, we met the challenge head on. The boy's trachea was filling with blood, blocking his airway. Without a clear airway, he would suffocate in a matter of minutes. Carlos tried desperately to insert a tube into the boy's airway so he could keep breathing. However, each time he tried to put the tube down the boy's throat, passing it between the vocal chords, all he could see was blood. It wasn't working, and we were losing precious time.

Carlos and I had company. Several people from a visiting church group work party had gathered in the doorway and were watching. Carlos kept trying to insert the tube, unsuccessfully.

Calling to the group, I said, "I need to ask you folks to leave. We've got a very sick young man." Actually, I was afraid the patient was going to die right before their eyes.

Carlos was dripping with sweat. I tried to suction the blood out of the boy's windpipe fast enough to give Carlos a clear look.

"There, it's in," he said finally. He had gotten the airway tube in place and the boy could breathe. Marty arrived in the operating theater and began administering curare, a drug that causes immediate muscle paralysis. This allowed Marty to give the boy a general anesthetic and ventilate him with oxygen.

By this time I had scrubbed my hands and put on a sterile gown and gloves. The surgical instruments were set up for a thoracotomy, so we could open his chest and remove part of the lung. "Dear Father in Heaven," I prayed silently with my eyes open as I surveyed the scene, "please work through us in helping to save this young man's life."

Steven and his helpers turned the young man on his right side and prepared him for surgery. By the time Carlos had scrubbed, I had made the long incision from the boy's spine in back nearly to his breastbone in front. I completed the cut to the inside of the chest cavity as air rushed in. We could see the lung expanding each time Marty squeezed the anesthesia bag. I could see and feel the heart rapidly beating below my bloody, gloved hands. Inserting the rib spreader, we cranked open the chest to improve the exposure. Then, working as quickly as we could, Carlos and I dissected the upper lobe of the left lung, separating it from the rest of the lung. Then, we tied heavy sutures around the large vessels which supplied blood to that part of the lung.

For the moment, the boy's life was literally in Marty's hands. As the hemorrhage into the boy's windpipe and out into the anesthesia tubing began to slow, Marty found he could ventilate the boy more effectively with his left hand, as he pumped blood into the boy's vein with his right. I was getting closer to the problem. Now, I could see the large bronchus, the passage way from the diseased lung to the windpipe. As I cut through it, air from the patient's airway blasted upward, spraying our faces with blood and fluid.

My glasses were peppered with red drops, but I had to keep going. As Carlos made the final cut, I lifted the TB-riddled lung out of the boy's chest and placed it in a metal basin. Quickly, I reached back into the depths of the chest cavity to hold the remaining lung out of the way. Unfortunately, Carlos didn't see me. He was busy closing up the bronchus. As my right hand returned, Carlos' hand swung upward with the instrument holding the large, curved needle that had just passed through the bronchus. The needle's tip caught my right index finger and would have passed completely through it had it not struck the bone.

I jerked my right hand back, feeling the pain. It was immediate and intense. The needle was stuck so deep in my finger that when I recoiled I lifted the needle, the needle holder, and Carlos' right hand.

"I'm sorry," Carlos said.

"It is okay," I responded, as I prayed to myself that it would be.

I got the needle out of my finger, but as I looked down I saw my glove finger begin to fill with blood. My blood! For a brief moment, I felt faint. I had now been stuck with a needle contaminated with the patient's blood. And because he was now receiving someone else's blood by transfusion, I could have hepatitis!

In the heat of the moment, I knew I had to keep going. I stood by as Carlos finished sewing up the bronchus, but we weren't finished yet. Together, we placed a chest tube through a small second incision to connect to a suction apparatus that would help to keep the collapsed lung expanded. Finally we closed the long incision.

Another surgery was completed, but my initiation into Tenwek Hospital was taking me right to the edge. I had been moments away from seeing a patient die. The sight of my own blood, filling up inside my once-sterile rubber glove, reminded me that even a physician is vulnerable to infection and disease, even in the act of bringing healing to a patient.

The young man did very well. By the third day after surgery, he was sitting outside the hospital with a wide smile on his face. He had lost part of a lung, and yet had found life in the process. Sometimes survival demands sacrifice, and only through sacrifice can one live. I didn't fully realize how profoundly Stanley had experienced this truth. I didn't really grasp what he had actually lost, and how much he gained, until he told me what really happened.

"I had dreams, Dr. Cheatham. I dreamed I could run faster than any other Kipsigis," said Stanley, who was lying on his side in his room at Tenwek the fifth day after his surgery. I had a few minutes after rounds and wanted to check on his condition.

"My dreams fell apart one day when I was playing soccer. I felt my leg snap twice and that was the end of me. My friends carried me to my family's hut where I stayed for the next two days."

"What did your leg feel like? How did you treat it?" I asked. The physician inside me wanted to know.

"We waited for the bush medicine doctor to come. It was my father's desire that he look at me."

I had heard enough about bush medicine to know that its "treatment," based on superstitions and folklore, bore no resemblance to modern medicine.

"The bush medicine doctor could not relieve my pain," Stanley continued. "He did not know what to do about the swelling or why my leg was discolored. He said it was broken and there was nothing he could do. The pain was intense, and I suffered greatly.

"Things got very silent, Dr. Cheatham, and then a voice from those who were crowded inside the hut said, 'Tenwek. Tenwek Hospital.' I could tell it was an elder. 'He must be taken to Tenwek Hospital! It is far away, but we can take him there.'

"Have you ever been transported twenty miles with a broken leg, Dr. Cheatham? My brothers, relatives, and friends carried me over dusty, rocky roads. With every step my friends took, I felt the pain vibrate through my fractured leg. I also knew I was one step closer to Tenwek. More than once the people who carried me nearly slipped and fell, but they held me up.

"We must have walked for some hours until we came to a road where cars and matatus would pass. Finally, a matatu stopped and I was placed in the back. Just me and twelve others, all in the back of a small truck that bounced from rut to pothole, large rock to ditch."

As Stanley talked, his face showed none of the pain he must have felt with each jolt and bump. And Stanley only glanced over the fact that every time he grimaced, his father hurt too. He hurt for his youngest son that he loved and knew would be taking care of him in his old age. He hurt knowing that the family still believed in bush medicine's curative powers. How could the white man's hospital heal his son?

"When the matatu took us that final mile up the road to Tenwek, my body was numb with pain. I remember seeing the sign *TENWEK HOSPITAL—WE TREAT, JESUS HEALS.* I did not know this Jesus.

"I became part of the long line of Kipsigis and Maasai waiting to enter the hospital grounds. After hours of bouncing, I was still, and I felt less pain, even though I was now surrounded by so many others who were injured or sick."

As Stanley spoke, I pictured all the patients, all the other "Stanley's" waiting outside Tenwek Hospital at that moment. I wondered what pain they had suffered to get there. Stanley described the American nurse who examined him, a missionary named Edna Boroff. I was told later that she had delivered some 18,000 babies. And I wondered how many nurses it would take to care for the patients now lined up, waiting to be admitted.

"Then, after they took an X-ray of my leg, I met a Dr. Ernest Steury." Stanley described how this thin, gentle, prematurely gray missionary doctor held the X-ray film in his left hand and extended his right hand in friendship.

"I looked in his eyes, Dr. Cheatham. I saw the same compassion I had seen in the eyes of the nurse. Dr. Steury told my father I had to enter the hospital. He explained the reason for the fracture, saying, 'There is evidence of a tumor in the bone.' He explained that the tumor had been present for some time and that it had been slowly eating away at the bone below the knee. The twist and the fall I took caused the diseased bone to break."

Stanley admitted the pronouncement of the slight, gray-haired doctor meant little to him and his family. "'A tumor, what is this tumor thing?' my father blurted out in Kipsigis." Stanley said. "Even before Dr. Steury could answer, I saw the serious look in his eyes. I felt my heart beating faster, and I became afraid.

"By now my leg was terribly swollen, and there was so much pain. I was given some medication and taken to the surgical ward, and there, for the first time, I began to relax."

I knew what was coming. I just couldn't anticipate the vivid way Stanley recalled the last hours before he lost his leg.

He described the two long rows of iron beds, each lined with a thin rubber mattress. He told me how he was placed on one and then felt the strangeness of the concrete block walls and corrugated metal roof. And he spoke of the odd floating sensation he felt in his head.

"I could feel myself becoming calm, because of the medicine Dr. Steury injected into my hip. But I was not prepared for what happened next. The sun had gone down, and as darkness filled the room, more patients began to come in from outdoors where they had spent the day. One of these was an elderly man. As he came closer and closer to my bed, I started to wonder. Then, I was at a total loss when he climbed into my narrow bed. Only then did I realize how many sick and injured patients there were.

"In the dark stillness of the ward, you could hear men breathing. It was as if each one retreated to the private space within himself. I looked out and saw so many eyes staring, roaming, and so many expressionless faces waiting in silence."

Stanley's story could have ended there, in the quiet preoccupation that preceded a deep sleep. But he kept going.

"It must have been late in the night when I saw a light and heard a familiar voice. 'Stanley, Stanley,' it said. 'It's Dr. Steury. I need to talk to you.'

"I sat up, and as my eyes cracked open I could see his tattered green surgical scrub suit and the crumpled surgical mask hanging around his neck. I could also tell my father was with him. What were they doing here at this hour? Dr. Steury spoke in Kipsigis, and he was very serious.

"He said, 'Stanley, the leg must be amputated. We must remove it if we are to try to save your life.'

"I could feel my body tremble. I stared at Dr. Steury and I did not believe him. No. No. No. I looked up and the light from the flashlight seemed to be reflected in Dr. Steury's eyes, through the tears that were forming.

"I would have kept staring ahead, Dr. Cheatham, if my father had not suddenly stepped forward. 'No, you will not cut off my son's leg! Removing his leg cannot have my permission. He must remain a complete man.' "

What Stanley didn't tell me, what I would soon learn, is that a son with one leg would be a terrible embarrassment to a father. His favorite son, his youngest son, who would look after him in his old age, would be a cripple with only one leg. And no amount of discussion was going to change the father's mind.

For the longest moment, Stanley said, his father stared at Dr. Steury. "Then he picked me up from the bed, my leg hanging painfully to the side, and he carried me out of the male ward, while I cried. He carried me out into the darkness of the night."

My few minutes with Stanley in-between rounds had lengthened into a half hour. And yet I could tell he was not ready to stop. I chose to keep listening, somewhat out of courtesy, but more out of an intense desire to know more.

"Dr. Cheatham, I know from Dr. Steury and the other missionary staff that my father took me from the hospital with my cancerous, fractured leg. They probably thought that once I returned to the bush, they would never hear from me again. Later I learned they had kept me in their prayers the whole time.

"All I remember is that two days later Dr. Steury was in the surgical theater performing an operation when someone told him I was waiting in the outpatient area. My mother and brothers had brought me back to Tenwek over those twenty craggy miles. When Dr. Steury found me, the pain felt terrible. 'Where is your father?' he wanted to know.

"My oldest brother, Philip, spoke up and said that a decision had been made that I would have the amputation as soon as possible. And then I told Dr. Steury that, once I was home, the pain was so great I cried constantly for two days."

I knew Dr. Steury had been in an awkward situation. Medically he knew what needed to be done. Stanley was ready for anything that would offer him some relief. Still, because the father objected so strongly, a feeling of reluctance was in the air, and everyone, especially Dr. Steury, could feel it. The bottom line was that Stanley's life was threatened. Dr. Steury decided to do the operation.

"I will never forget those last hours before surgery," said Stanley. "I could feel my body becoming more and more anxious. That's about the time I saw him."

"Him?" I asked.

"David Kilel, the chaplain at Tenwek. He was a quiet, dignified man, filled with a compassionate spirit. His look, his caring and concern were like I had seen in the nurse and in Dr. Steury. I recognized him immediately. He was from the area near my home. In fact, I could recall that David's younger brother, John, was in my initiation rite. For that reason alone I felt I was with a friend in this worst moment of my life.

"David talked to me about Tenwek. He told me it was a place 'where the healing power of Jesus is available to those who would accept Him as their Lord and Savior, and who would give their lives to Him.'

"Then he opened his large, black Bible, and read to me from the 23rd Psalm: 'The Lord is my shepherd, I shall not want.'

"You know, Dr. Cheatham, I had been a shepherd. I did not know this Lord that David was talking about, but I knew what it meant to care for one's sheep.

"Then he continued to read. And as he did, I pictured the shepherd: 'He makes me to lie down in green pastures. He leads me beside the still waters. He restores my soul. He leads me in the paths of righteousness for His name's sake. Yea though I walk through the valley of the shadow of death, I will fear no evil, for You are with me. Your rod and Your staff, they comfort me. You prepare a table before me in the presence of my enemies. You anoint my head with oil. My cup runs over. Surely goodness and mercy shall follow me all the days of my life, and I will dwell in the house of the Lord forever.'

"I looked over at my mother, and in her eyes I could see approval as David finished reading. Then David bowed his head and talked to God, just like He was right there in the room. He prayed for me, Dr. Cheatham. I remember his words. 'God, we pray for loving mercy and healing power during surgery. And we pray that Stanley might accept Jesus Christ as his personal Savior.'

"At that moment, I felt so frightened. At the same time, I felt strangely calmed as they wheeled me into the operating theater. Once inside, I remember I was draped with a sheet, and then they injected me with something to ease the pain.

"My body continued to shiver. My eyes were wide with fear. I was breathing so fast I couldn't count how fast my heart was pounding. As I glanced up, a Kipsigis attendant we call the "medicine giver" applied a rubber tourniquet to my upper arm. He wiped the skin with some cold liquid and then thrust a needle into a bulging vein. I saw a long clear tube connected to a bottle of water hanging over my head. And then I saw my family leave the room. I knew what they were feeling. I knew that, now, I was all alone.

"Dr. Steury . . . I remember Dr. Steury and the way he explained the surgery. His voice was warm and caring. He said, 'This is what we're going to do, and this is why we're doing it.' And as he talked, my fear began to fade. You remember me telling you about that floating sensation I felt on my first trip to the hospital?"

"Yes," I said.

"I could feel the same thing, because a feeling of total relaxation overcame me. I asked Dr. Steury several questions about surgery, and one thing he said still stands out: 'If the surgery is not done, death would occur due to spread of the bone cancer throughout the body.'

"Instead of frightening me, his words actually gave me great calm. I finally believed this was the right decision. Then, with everything ready, Dr. Steury said, 'Let us pray.' I saw him bow his head and close his eyes. He seemed to be talking to someone who was not there. Yet as he talked, it was as if someone *were* present. And it was someone Dr. Steury knew very well. While he prayed, I closed my eyes, and I wondered if I could see this same God and talk with Him.

"The mild sedation made me feel I was a spectator at my own operation. Although I could feel nothing in my leg, I could see movements reflected in the glass face of the large overhead operating room light. I could see blood—my blood. I could hear voices, low and somewhat muffled. And I could hear the unmistakable sound of the rasping movements of a saw as it was pulled back and forth.

"But what I remember most was the way Dr. Steury would lean over the screen and ask me how I was doing. It was the most reassuring thing.

"I don't know if you have ever lain on an operating table during surgery, Dr. Cheatham. I looked up and I could see through the windows. I could see birds flying, unconcerned about the great loss I was feeling. I could hear people outside. I could hear children playing. It was hard to believe what was happening to me while, just a few feet away, life was continuing for others."

What goes through the mind of a young man who knows he is losing his leg? I wondered.

"As I lay on that table, I thought of all the things I had desired most in life. Wealth. Power. Women. These things fueled my passion, Dr. Cheatham. They were the reasons I woke up in the morning, and why I would let no person deny me. But as I thought about these things that had burned so deeply in my heart, I felt a fire dying. I thought of what I was about to lose, my leg, my ability to walk and run.

"I thought, 'What else could I lose?' And then, a new thought, a new feeling began to come over me: What if I gained all the power and the possessions in the land where I lived? It would mean nothing to me if I lost my life. It was then that I remembered David Kilel telling me about what had happened to him inside. And it all began to make sense.

"The minutes that followed were difficult ones for Dr. Steury. I know because he told me. After surgery, word came to Dr. Steury that my father had just arrived at the hospital and was waiting outside. Dr. Steury was just putting in the final stitches, and he said he could not help but feel frightened at the thought of walking out of the operating room where he would be confronted by my father. He feared that my father would be very angry because of what had been done to me.

"So he prayed for guidance and strength, and he went outside to meet my family. What happened next came as a complete surprise to Dr. Steury. My father reached out his hand to Dr. Steury in a very warm greeting. He said, 'I have come to offer my word of agreement that Stanley's leg needed to be removed. I have great love for my son. Because of this love, I ask you to do whatever is necessary to care for him.'

"I did not hear much more than that. My heart was so moved by my father. He and Dr. Steury still talked as the nurses wheeled me on a gurney cart down the hall. I knew my family was walking behind me. When we came to the surgical ward, they helped move me into my bed.

"Looking down the bed, I could see my right leg, but my left one was missing. I was overcome with a feeling of deep sadness. One by one, my father, my mother, and my brothers gathered to stand near my bed. This was my family, the people who loved me. I cannot describe the comfort that came to me inside, nor the feeling of despair that hung over me like a cloud. My body had betrayed me and my father and my family as well.

"I looked into all their faces, Dr. Cheatham, and I felt like a child—a child in deep need of his family. And I would have stayed like that had not a deeper need welled up inside me. It came from somewhere in my heart. That is all I can say. David Kilel came to my bedside, and the words jumped from my mouth: 'The Lord has saved my life. He has safely carried me through the operation.'

"Then I took David's hand. 'I am now accepting Jesus Christ, God's Son, as my Savior, and I will always follow Him.'"

I had heard these words. I knew what they meant to me. And I could tell, as Stanley recounted the events in his hospital room, that this new declaration of faith sprang from deep inside him, from the realization that his life was being made new. Somewhere between his former passions and the tiny hospital room where he lay after surgery, something had changed.

"That night, Dr. Cheatham, that first night in the hospital, was so long. I could not sleep. I would open my weary, tear-filled eyes and I could see the faint moonlight streaming in through the window. I could see it mirrored in the eyes of my father who stood faithfully at my bed. As the medication and the effects of the spinal anesthetic wore off, I looked at myself. I saw again that part of me was missing, and I knew I would be that way forever. I was no longer a complete man! In such a short span of time, my life, my plans, my ambitions for greatness had changed. At least the agonizing pain in my leg was not so bad. But a greater pain remained inside.

"It must have been very late when fatigue finally overcame me and I fell asleep. My father remained at my bedside throughout the long hours of darkness. His heart was filled with grief. He must have seen the outline of my body, lying beneath the thick blanket, and he could see the form of one very long leg and where my other leg used to be.

"I know my father. I know at that moment he was wondering how his son would manage with only one leg. How would I be accepted back in the village now that I was a cripple?

"Those questions kept him awake as the night turned into morning. And that was when I truly woke up to the reality I lived with. I remember the first rays of sun coming through the window, and I remember turning suddenly onto my left side. My good leg, the right one, hit what remained of my left leg. I felt a sharp bolt of pain from my wound race through my hip. I wanted to roll back and sit up all at once. I wanted to cry, but the reserve that had been born into my body silenced my suffering.

"My eyelids squeezed tight. My teeth clenched. I could feel the muscles of my jaws almost spasm as I twisted my head to the side and buried my face in the thin pillow. My forehead and upper lip broke out with perspiration. I couldn't hold back.

"'Ayeeeeeee!' As I screamed inside, I kept my eyes closed. I didn't want to see what I knew was no longer there. I moved my right leg out as far as it would go. I pressed the foot and each of my toes against the cold metal end of the bed. I tried to do the same with the left leg, and what I still thought was my foot. But there was only more pain in my shortened thigh.

"I raised my head and shoulders and slowly, so slowly, I opened my eyes and looked down at the leg that wasn't there. What had been the left limb, at mid-thigh, ceased to exist. I knew it was only a bad dream. A nightmare that had become a reality.

"My left leg was truly gone. I was no longer whole."

As Stanley spoke, I took in every word, picturing the young man, ten years earlier, who now lay once again inside Tenwek Hospital. Stanley paused for a second, as if returning to that exact moment in the story he recounted with vivid detail. Then he continued to revisit the moment, without a hint of pain.

"All I could do was close my eyes. Then I lay back down and felt smothered by a blanket of despair. I felt a hand on my left shoulder. It was a powerful grip. I looked up and there was my father. His face showed no expression, yet his eyes were damp and they shown through the tears. When my father touched me, he touched my emotions. He kept me still. He stayed with me as I realized my loss.

"While my father remained, David Kilel came in the doorway of the surgical ward. I could see the big, black book under his arm, the same book he had read from the day before. 'David, please read to me again, about the valley, the valley where there is no fear.'

"He began to read to me. He read stories of how Jesus healed the sick. You have read those stories, I am sure, haven't you?"

"Yes, I have read them," I said.

"Then, you believe that miracles are possible?"

"Yes, I do, Stanley. You can't explain miracles, yet they are real, aren't they?"

"Yes, Dr. Cheatham."

I can't explain how Stanley Cheborge, aware that he now had cancer, had so much life inside. But it was real. I would be staying a little more than five additional weeks in his world. How long he would hold on to life I didn't know. I just knew I didn't want him to leave.

SEVEN

Surgical instruments and patient beds were in short supply at Tenwek. So was sleep. On most days it came late in the day, when my last patient visits ended around 10:00 p.m. Once back inside our one-room dwelling I was good for only another thirty minutes—time to eat a bowl of soup and have some scattered conversation with the family. By the time I fell into bed, the night seemed absolutely still. I was sure no doctor's paging service could find me there. I remember the evening I was wrong.

Sylvia heard the noise first. "Mel, wake up! Mel!" Her urgent whispers pulled me out of a deep sleep. "Someone's at the front door."

I was almost coherent. Sit up. Listen. It sounded like impatient knuckles on wood—polite tapping that grew into loud knocks. It was late. I couldn't imagine who was standing on our doorstep, but I was sure it had to be an emergency.

I threw myself out of bed and followed the knocking sounds to the front door. "Mel, I'm sorry to do this." The unbridled drawl belonged to Shaw Yount, a short-term World Medical Mission volunteer physician from North Carolina.

"Shaw, what's going on?"

He raised his right hand and held up an X-ray. "Mel, would you look at this and see if you think it's osteomyelitis?"

I squinted my eyes up at the one dim bulb outside our door. The scant light gave shape to the film's milky-white tones.

"It doesn't look like any X-ray I've ever seen," I said.

"It's not," said Shaw. "It's an X-ray of a dog's leg. It's Poodaroo's left paw."

Poodaroo was a mixture of several kinds of dog. He certainly was not a purebred. He had belonged to Carlos and Claudia Somoza, who had given him to Shaw. The name "Poodaroo," which is Spanish for "popcorn," had always humored me. Until now. What was I doing standing on the front step in my pajamas, late at night, looking at an X-ray of a dog's leg? I was beginning to wake up in a hurry.

"What do you think it is, Mel?"

I held up the X-ray to the light, again, and could see a small questionable shadow along the bone of his left forepaw. "I can't tell what it is, Shaw. It looks to me like Poodaroo has either stepped on a thorn or been bitten by a snake."

"He's limping and in a lot of pain, Mel. I really think there's infection in the bone." Shaw's lazy drawl was growing more urgent by the second.

"Well, what do you think we ought to do, Shaw?"

"I think you ought to operate on Poodaroo. I think you need to drain the pus in the bone like you would any child."

Poodaroo's owner was serious. At this hour, the hospital was dark. All of Tenwek was in bed. I looked at Shaw and wondered if he knew it was now almost midnight.

"Let me have a look at it in the morning," I said.

"You think it can wait that long?" he asked.

I knew Shaw had great compassion for people. And for dogs, as well. I assured Shaw that Poodaroo would be all right until the next day, even if he needed surgery. With nervous reluctance, Shaw agreed. As he ambled back to his quarters, still clutching the X-ray, I knew I'd be adding one more operation to the next day's schedule.

The next morning, after a light breakfast of Kenyan corn flakes, I was back in the operating theater. There were about a dozen surgeries on the list for that day. Within a few minutes I saw Shaw poke his head in.

"How's it going today, Mel?" he asked.

Every couple of hours Shaw was back. "How busy are you Mel? When do we get to Poodaroo?"

The operation will probably be a breeze, I thought. It was Shaw's health I had begun to worry about.

Morning rolled into afternoon, then into evening. We had just wrapped up the last scheduled surgery. Only one more operation remained, but there was one problem: the patient was a dog. This meant we couldn't use the main operating room. If any Kipsigis hospital staff walked in and saw that our patient had four legs, they might not understand.

We brought Poodaroo into the old operating room, a small area off the main operating theater, which was being used to apply plaster casts to broken limbs. Bob Byers, an anesthesiologist from Yuba City, California, and a few nurses from a visiting work crusade served as our team. We sat Poodaroo on the table.

"I hope he does all right," Shaw said. "I just know we can't leave him like this, and not try to help him." Poodaroo looked nervous and apprehensive, too. He seemed to sense that something unusual was about to take place, and that it involved him. Bob Byers injected some Ketamine into his leg. Normally, a person will go out in less than one minute. After five minutes, however, Poodaroo was still sitting up and looking around. I gave him another cc of the anesthesia. Finally, after several more injections of various medications, Poodaroo shut his eyes.

I shaved his left front paw. Then, I made an incision and drained the pus. Now things would be better.

All this time, Shaw's eyes were wide open as he stroked Poodaroo's fur. "How is it going, Mel?" His voice had the edge of a nervous father. I realized, again, how much I admired Shaw. I don't think I've ever met a more caring person.

"There," I said confidently wrapping the paw in a large white bandage. "Poodaroo is going to live." Shaw, himself, had even survived. As I took off my gloves I looked over at Shaw and said, "Poodaroo should wake up in another thirty minutes." After two hours the dog hadn't moved a muscle. Another hour went by. Shaw's face was shrouded in doubt. I was becoming more and more concerned.

The nurses left. I cleaned up. Bob Byers said good bye. And with his anxiety meter rising to a new level, Shaw hovered over his dog, who was still in a deep sleep. Things were serious. As I left the cast room, I turned to look back and saw Shaw standing next to his beloved Poodaroo. And both were absolutely quiet.

That night, somewhere in the dark Kenyan sky, people awoke to the rise and fall of a siren. This seemed puzzling to visiting Americans, since there were no ambulances at Tenwek. The sound came over the rooftops from the other side of the compound—from the direction where Shaw lived! The siren was Poodaroo! At 3:00 a.m. he was howling non-stop. Strange as it seemed, his night song made sense: Ketamine, the anesthesia used in the surgery, is hallucinatory. A large patient like Poodaroo had required a large dose. Now, Poodaroo was coming down from a bad trip! For three hours he howled. The good news was, he had finally woken up. Unfortunately, the next day, some at Tenwek were only half-awake.

I got the whole story early that morning before surgery when I made my house call to see Poodaroo. His owner was unshaven, worried, and still very much concerned. Shaw looked at me, twenty-four hours of restless fatigue etched into his brow. "Mel," he said, "do you think Poodaroo will always be like this?" I looked down at the big shaggy, yellow dog. As he tried to walk, both his front and back limbs went cross-legged. Poor Poodaroo. In an awkward two-step shuffle, he tried to walk, then his wobbly, furry frame collapsed in a heap. As much as I was tempted, I didn't dare laugh. Shaw was beyond humor. He needed the assurance of a physician. "Shaw, I think Poodaroo will be just fine," I said, as the dog struggled unsuccessfully to stand on all fours. That afternoon, the dog was running around on his bandaged paw. Later in the evening I stopped by Poodaroo's to give Shaw a house call of his own. He was smiling like his old self. "Great job, doctor. The patient is making an excellent recovery."

I looked over at the dog's contented face. Whatever he thought about his hurt paw, the late night howling, or the doctor who had operated on him, Poodaroo was grinning at me. And I could tell he held no grudge.

Tenwek Hospital needed more Poodaroo's. Treating sick patients offered few daily opportunities for laughter. And for good reason. I remember the two-year-old girl I operated on. She had burns over 40 percent of her body. After accidentally falling into her family's open pit fire, she faced several weeks of tedious, torturous, skin grafts.

The ordeal of a burned child was hard not to notice. Other expressions of pain were not as obvious. These people had learned to live with discomfort. There was no announcement, no visible hint of the hurt inside. There was the twenty-six-year-old Maasai man who had a huge parasitic cyst in his abdominal cavity. He looked like a pregnant woman ready to deliver. The growth that Dr. Wesche and I removed weighed eighteen pounds. Yet even though the incision extended from his lower rib cage to his pelvic area, this man was sitting upright in bed the day after surgery. The pain had to be excruciating, although you would never have guessed it.

Only when a Kipsigis suffered an injury and displayed an operative wound could I glimpse how deep their suffering went. I remember the seventy-year-old man who had received a blood transfusion following a prostatectomy. The bed literally shook as he lay on his back wracked by an attack of malaria that had been brought on by a blood transfusion. His pain was controlled with Tylenol.

These were my patients, and each time I learned about their particular pain I asked myself the same question, "How did this happen?" Sometimes the cause was medical: A tumor in a lung that needed to be removed. A broken femur that required a cast. An obstructed bowel that could be unblocked with surgery. As a physician, I knew these problems were treatable. I knew how to anticipate, plan, and execute a successful surgery. In the many instances where I seemed to lack knowledge or experience, God seemed to provide both. Even with limited equipment and supplies, with the risk of infection higher than in a modern U.S. hospital, Tenwek's patients recovered. Their wounds healed. Their smiles returned. They went back to their homes to farm, eat, and live.

But there were other questions I couldn't ignore. These were questions that always began and ended with Why? Why, for example, were there so many parasites in the drinking water? I remembered Franklin Graham's often-uttered observation that "More people die from polluted water in this world than from anything else." And there were other Whys? Why, after years of painful injuries, were Kipsigis children still falling into cooking fires in the middle of their familys' huts? I could order medication that would remove worms from a person's digestive track. However, I couldn't remove the Kipsigis' century-old habit of drinking polluted water. Yet, as a physician, I often thought of the frequent miscarriages, probably brought on by lack of proper diet and prenatal care. I thought of the many babies born prematurely, probably the result of the mother contracting malaria or other infections. And there was the frequency of TB, measles, polio, and hepatitis that could be greatly reduced if the people learned and practiced better public health.

Sometimes such health dangers became the ironic catalyst for an innovative solution that benefited the entire community. Tenwek's community health program, for instance, had designed a raised hearth fireplace to prevent small children from stumbling into an open flame and needlessly being burned. Several years after its introduction, the raised hearth fireplace has significantly reduced the number of burn patients.

Tenwek, I soon learned, was home to other Whys that had no satisfying answers. The farmer with inoperable cancer. The woman with progressive kidney failure. The teenage boy with a strange progressive disease that defied diagnosis, yet developed into a coma, then death. When a family member asked, "What can you do, doctor?" I could only say, "There is nothing more we can do but pray for improvement." The look on the person's face would still ask, "Why? Why is this happening to me?"

As a neurosurgeon I had been trained to help people and maybe save a life by performing delicate operations on the human brain and spinal cord. In spite of all my medical training and experience and my ability to make moment-by-moment, life-saving decisions, I still could not answer a patient's perplexing question, "Why me?"

Each time we returned to Tenwek, I asked myself the same questions: Am I really making a difference? Is being here in this hiccup-of-an-outpost on the far side of the world making a significant blip on the screen? Does any of my work really matter?

These questions would sit on my shoulder and whisper to me as I walked past the rows of sick patients during early-morning rounds. I would wonder which child would be at risk because we were desperately short of antibiotics. And that's when I met a person like Kipkoech.

He was a little Kipsigis boy of seven. One day he suddenly appeared on the pediatrics ward with swelling in several areas of his scalp. In four or five places I could see pus draining out. Dr. Susie Cheatham, our daughter-in-law who, along with our son Michael, had just graduated from Vanderbilt Medical School, had obtained an X-ray which showed multiple areas of osteo-myelitis of the skull. Osteomyelitis is infection in the bone.

I remember Michael helping me operate on this little boy like it was yesterday. I removed the skull in several places and large amounts of pus drained from the bone in other places. It was obvious that his problem was chronic. Completing the surgery, I wondered what it would be like to be seven years old and to have had surgery. I saw Kipkoech shortly after the operation. He wore a cap which covered the bandage on his head.

In the next few days, Kipkoech surprised me. He wouldn't leave me alone. It seemed that wherever I turned, he would be standing in front of me, flashing a big, wide grin. He would extend his right hand, palm upward, and say the two words of English someone had taught him: "Gimme fauve!" I would oblige by giving him five, slapping my palm down against his. This was just a warm up, as he sought out other missionary staff who might "gimme fauve." Kipkoech learned more English words. He came through the hospital days later, looked at me and said, "Jesus lawes me."

I never did see a mother or father who seemed to belong to Kipkoech. Before operating on him, I had asked for his parents. A boy, perhaps in his teens, appeared and announced he was "the relative" and that there was "no parent to come."

Now I knew why Stanley wanted to start an orphanage. So far as I knew, Kipkoech's parents were not alive. If so, this young boy would be taken in by other family members, but I didn't know for sure.

One thing I knew: if I remained at Tenwek, I would probably see Kipkoech again when he was older, because of some injury or a worsening of his skull infection or infection somewhere else in his body. In fact, that week, I had already seen the future of this little boy. Give him a few more years, I thought, and he might be a teenager with a bowel obstruction. Let him grow up and avoid hepatitis, and he might be carried into Tenwek as the man who had fallen from an overcrowded matatu. Allow him to grow old and this smiling seven-year-old could one day be the elderly man suffering from stomach cancer.

I looked at Kipkoech resting on the same bed with two other children, and I asked myself, "Are you making any difference, Mel?" I would probably never know the answer. However, I was sure of one thing: I was busy working in the place where God had called me, and with faith, this knowledge was enough for me.

Faith meant walking into Stanley Cheborge's room when I knew a malignant tumor was growing inside of him.

"Dr. Cheatham, you have come back once again! I have something to read you. It is from Matthew 4:23: 'Jesus went throughout Galilee, teaching in their synagogues, preaching the good news of the kingdom, and healing every disease and sickness among the people.'"

I thought back to Stanley's story of growing up proud and strong and so confident in his ability to run and impress others. I remember the words he had shared with me the day before, the words he had spoken during the first dark hours after his amputation. The person lying in bed, beaming with confidence, was not the same brash athlete who previously had enjoyed so much pleasure with women. This was not the loud, dominant man who needed to be in control. Something had happened inside him. I did not know the entire story. Yet.

"After the surgery, David Kilel placed a Bible at my bedside. I began to read it. And I didn't stop reading. I started to talk with other patients. I wanted to know more about Jesus.

"One day, as Dr. Steury was changing my dressing, I said, 'Isn't it wonderful that God brought me to Tenwek Hospital so that you could cut off my bad leg and save my life?' "

I could not pretend to imagine the ordeal that still lay ahead of him. His amputation stump healed, and he was well enough to ride in a matatu back to Lelaitich.

"I was now a cripple. I would never run fast or be a great leader. I would just be pitied as only part of a man."

"What was it like for you going back home, Stanley?"

"As the vehicle slowed to cross a mud hole, I could see some friends from my village. I dropped my head. I could not look at them. When I glanced down, I noticed the crumpled up pieces of paper David Kilel had written on and given to me back at the hospital. They were Bible words that talked about the 'newness of life': 'Therefore, if anyone is in Christ, he is a new creation; old things have passed away; behold all things have become new!' (2 Cor. 5:17). I didn't know what it meant to have the Lord make someone a new person.

"My brothers were there to greet me when the matatu stopped. They helped me lie down on the hard mud floor of my family's thatched-roof hut. And that's when I knew I was home."

I expected Stanley to break out into one of his patented smiles, but his face was filled with thought, as if he were back inside his family's hut, surrounded by wall-to-wall earth.

"I did not know what it meant to be dependent upon others, to count on my family and friends for almost everything. I needed them to stand up, to eat, to make sure I had water to drink. I did not know what it would be like to learn to walk again. I had no crutch. I used a six-foot-long tree limb to propel myself by placing it ahead and hopping forward on my one foot."

Stanley paused, as if feeling the weight of the last ten years since the amputation. "I never felt so helpless. Yet up to that point in life I had never been so fortunate."

"What do you mean?" I asked.

"You have heard these words I'm sure: 'Whoever desires to save his life will lose it, and whoever loses his life for My sake will save it.' (Luke 9:24). Dr. Steury had told me before surgery that I might lose my life if my cancerous leg was not removed. My leg was lost, yet my life was saved—not by me, nor by Dr. Steury. My life was no longer my own. I now belonged to the One who had saved me from death.

"I knew the words David Kilel had taken from the Bible were meant for me: 'For God so loved the world that He gave His only begotten Son, that whoever believes in Him should not perish but have everlasting life.' (John 3:16). They were Jesus' words: 'Most assuredly, I say to you, unless one is born of water and the Spirit, he cannot enter the Kingdom of God' (John 3:5).

"When I read these words. I knew I must be baptized. I wanted a new life as a servant of Jesus Christ." Stanley could have ended the story there. But there was more he wanted to say.

"When I told my mother I wanted to be baptized, she told me this was her desire, too. Ever since the death of my brother, Kipketwol, earlier, she wanted to declare her faith. But I will never forget this event because of where we went.

"My mother and I were taken by the pastor to a place on the river called Mengit. The body of rushing, muddy water looked familiar and took me back to the events of two years earlier. This was the site of my initiation, the place of so much struggle and pain, the dark waters where my brother had died. But this time was different. This time, I was not alone. Two friends supported me on each side. Lower and lower I sank.

With the water almost up to my chin, I heard the pastor say, 'I baptize you in the name of the Father, the Son, and the Holy Spirit.'

"I opened my eyes, and all I could see was murky, dark shapes. But the water ran off. As I emerged from the river I was not the same. Something inside me was different. Something inside me was being born. I was being born again. I was emerging from the water with new life in the exact spot where I had been initiated into manhood!

"Once the river had brought pain. Now it was a symbol of new life. The waters of my Christian baptism physically symbolized that my sins had been washed away by the blood of Jesus Christ. Losing my leg was no longer a handicap. It was a reminder to me that I could no longer stand on my own. The younger 'powerful' Stanley had died. I would keep living, but no longer for myself. From now on, I would live for the One who saved me, Jesus Christ."

As I listened to Stanley's story, my mind flashed back to my own youth in Kansas. I remembered how I had grown up in the church, and had listened to my mother tell me Bible stories during the evening. As an adult, I had taught Sunday school for two years. I had served on the board of elders. Still, all of the worship services and committees couldn't answer the question God was asking me: "What have you done for Me?" I didn't know how to answer this. I wasn't sure I *had* an answer.

I had role models of faith early in life, pastors like Ed Wright, professional peers like Dr. Williamson and Dr. Brackett. Now, I was in my fifties, and wondering what I would say to the Lord when I stood before Him and He asked me, "What have you done for Me?"

What would I say? "I was willing to lose six weeks of income to go to Tenwek Hospital. I operated on a special, young Kipsigis man who showed me the meaning of faith."

That's when I looked back at Stanley and thought about what he had already lost. His leg. His pride. And yet he had what I desired but somehow lacked—a seemingly limitless capacity to trust God and live his life for Him.

This is why I stayed a little longer whenever I went into Stanley's room. My visits weren't just a doctor asking his patient how he felt. It was two men, from entirely different worlds, each with something to give the other. Logic said that if I stayed with Stanley long enough to share his world, his journey, his pain, a part of me would remain in Kenya. I did not realize it at the time, but this is exactly what was happening.

"You said after you were baptized, the loss of your leg was no longer a handicap," I said to Stanley.

"That is right, because I now had something to live for, Jesus Christ. I wanted to go back to school. My father, however, had different plans. He met with the elders of the tribe and decided that I needed a wife, and that one would be found for me. 'I am planning for someone to take care of you,' he told me. 'A dowry of several cows has been offered to the parents of the bride.'

"I told my father 'No. I am now a Christian, and I cannot marry a girl who is not a Christian. God is calling me to school, so that I can learn and make my life one of serving others.'

"My father erupted. 'There is not a God. Therefore I am god! It was I who brought you into the world, and that makes me your god!'

" 'No, father, you are wrong,' I said. 'You are my father, and I love you, but you are not God.' This was one of the most painful things I had ever experienced in life. Kipsigis children do not say these things to their parents. But I had to say these things to remain faithful as a follower of Jesus."

I looked at Stanley and said, "I have never had to make the choice you made, the choice between choosing your parents and choosing God. You made an extremely difficult decision."

"I made the only choice I could, because I could not turn my back on the One who had given me a second chance to live."

Then, Stanley's story took a wide turn, twenty-five miles beyond his father's anger and his family's hut to the Kabungut Secondary School, where he attended after he lost his leg. "My friends did not know me. They wanted to know, 'Can this be the person we knew and feared?' They knew how cunning and mean I could be. I had to laugh, and tell them, yes, I was still Stanley, but that I was different."

The difference showed after he applied for a transfer to Tenwek School. Someone asked Stanley if he would teach a Sunday school class at Aisaik. By saying Yes, Stanley had to wake up at five o'clock on Sunday morning in order to walk seven miles—on a crutch!

"Those were dry, dusty, lonely roads," he said. "I had time to think, time to realize I had been given a new chance to live. I wasn't the center of attention anymore. Instead of playing soccer, I became a spectator. I saw people playing and winning as a team, rather than as individuals. This was all new to me.

"I became a spectator of life. I began to ask, 'Where did I come from? Why am I here?' Over the next several months I began to discover the answers. After I graduated, I enrolled in Kericho Highlands Bible College. Inside I felt this urgency about life. The Lord had something important for me to do, and I had to find out what it was."

Part of the answer, Stanley told me, was a person, Annah Chumo. The two had met when they were students at Kabungut Secondary School. Quiet and reserved, Annah was almost in direct contrast to Stanley's gregarious, exuberant nature. Stronger than their differences was their shared faith, their call to full-time Christian work. They courted and fell in love. Finally, after eight months of waiting and after both graduated from Bible college, they married.

"So many people came to the wedding, it was impossible to crowd everyone inside the small, rural church building. People were sitting on the lawn," Stanley remembered. As he replayed the day in his mind, I understood why he remembered so much. The ceremony lasted two hours, and Stanley stood the entire time. Surgery back in the U.S. had kept Dr. Steury, Stanley's close friend, from officiating at the ceremony. As Dr. Wesche performed the wedding, Stanley stood without relief, balancing his weight on one leg that was warm and alive and another that was cold and artificial. Then he felt twinges of pain, not in what remained of his left leg, but in his good leg.

"At the time I thought it was because I was standing so long," Stanley said, his voice trailing off.

After the couple were married, and he was working as an assistant pastor at the Kericho Africa Gospel Church, Stanley said his heart and mind were focused on only one thing.

"I kept thinking about Jesus as He healed people who were sick. Their pain and suffering was now much more real to me after I lost my leg. And I thought about others Jesus wanted to touch. These were not just the people in the Bible. They were the widows, the orphans, the sick in the area where I lived."

As Stanley talked, as his words intensified and his eyes widened, I knew I was listening in on a major chapter of his life story.

"God gave me the vision to build an orphanage, a retirement home for elderly widows, and eventually a hospital. I knew how Tenwek Hospital and School had grown from a small out-post mission station. I thought of the Londiani area, far to the north of my home. It had just as many poor people. The need for health care and for people to receive Jesus Christ were both great.

"I had heard Dr. Steury tell about Franklin Graham, the president of Samaritan's Purse, and how the Lord had worked through him to bring doctors and nurses and equipment to

Tenwek. That's why I could picture a hospital in Londiani as a place where physicians from developed countries could come as short-term volunteers. They could teach and train Kenyan physicians. Modern medical care could become a reality for more of the Kenyan people, couldn't it?"

"Yes, it could," I said.

"I knew this would be humanly impossible, especially for a cripple," he said. "I began using my old crutch again because of the new pain I was feeling in my good leg. I could not give up, though."

"Why?" I asked.

"Because one evening my vision came alive. I was singing in chapel, when I came to the words of the chorus, 'He that overcomes shall stand.' My eyes fell to the floor and I saw my crutch lying on the floor. Then, I raised my head and began singing from deep down. I remembered how God had helped me overcome my pain. I thought if He could give me new life, He could also help me overcome the obstacles that stood in the way of helping the widow, the orphan, and the sick."

It was a watershed moment of faith. Stanley took his dream to high places in the Kenyan government. He showed them the area where the project could be built, and what it would mean to many, many of the area's poor who went without.

"I decided I had to use everything God had given me. For years I had learned to trade grain and cattle with the Maasai. I used those bargaining powers to get officials' support. I used my height, my toothy grin, my manner, my voice. And I also decided to use patience. I traveled back and forth from my hut to government offices, more miles than they thought I could endure. Finally, my efforts reached the top levels of Kenyan government. I asked for twenty-five acres of land to be donated for this home for widows, orphans, and the sick. When I opened the envelope I was surprised. I was not given twenty-five acres. They had decided to give fifty acres! Hope was turning into a reality."

So was the pain in Stanley's right hip. The slight discomfort on his wedding day grew more disturbing. Stanley needed relief for his joints, money for the project, and perseverance to see the plan grow. All three were almost nil from the start. When his enthusiasm began to grow, so did the soreness in his right hip. The slight limp became a pronounced hitch.

"The pain stopped everything. I ceased traveling. Within a few weeks, the vision that was once so clear, faded like a mirage in the hot sun. I felt just like the artificial leg I had worn for the past eight years; I creaked and groaned with each step. I needed more than a new leg. I needed to know that God was still walking by my side.

"Dr. Teeter, a surgeon from Pennsylvania, measured me for a new leg, a brown one, that would be brought by a visiting doctor from America." Stanley grinned at me, and I saw his life coming full circle.

"You believe patience is a virtue, don't you, Dr. Cheatham?"

"Yes, why?"

"Patience has not come easily to me. After I knew the new leg was coming, I waited. The pain in my lower spine started going down my right leg. I could only pray that God would bring the new leg fast, and that it would bring an end to all that hurt within me."

In my mind I saw the large, chocolate brown leg our family had brought with us on the plane from Ventura. It was standing in the corner of Stanley's room. It had provided no physical comfort for Stanley. At this point I wondered what, if anything, would.

"Dr. Cheatham, there is one question I still cannot answer."

"What's that?"

"What is going to happen to my body in this earthly life?"

"Since we couldn't remove all of the tumor, it will continue to grow. You will experience more pain and more weakness and numbness." As a physician, I had a responsibility to tell Stanley exactly what he faced. Whatever emotions I felt for him were secondary to the truth. And the truth was he was dying.

"Maybe this is the case. Maybe I will be healed," Stanley responded.

"There's the possibility I could arrange radiation therapy and chemotherapy for you in Nairobi."

"Maybe, Dr. Cheatham. Maybe. . ."   Stanley seemed open to the treatment, although I could tell, as we talked more, his heart was set on going home.

"Tomorrow, Dr. Graber has agreed to drive me back to my village in his car. I will see you then, won't I?"

"Yes, you will Stanley." As much as I wanted to assure him more, I had run out of words. In less than forty-eight hours, I had successfully operated on a dog and monitored the recovery of his owner. I had seen several patients cling to life and survive. And I had walked beside a friend whose pain I hardly envied, but whose faith humbled me to the core.

Soon he was traveling home. He had started the twisted, rocky twenty-mile journey to Lelaitich in the front passenger seat. By the time the van reached the main gate of the hospital compound, Stanley was in great pain.

Just before the combi pulled away, Stanley called back to me. "Will you and your family come to visit me in my home before you leave Kenya?"

"Yes," I called. "We will come."

Then the van rolled out through the main entrance of the hospital and into a cloud of diesel dust. I waved goodbye. I had every intention of seeing Stanley at his family's hut. I wanted to make good on this promise, just like Stanley had pledged to build the orphanage. Now, however, I saw fifty acres of hope lying fallow. And I knew that fulfilling Stanley's dream would soon be left to someone else. For sick patients like him and orphans like Kipkoech, who still had so much life to live, someone else would need to take on Stanley's dream.

EIGHT

When does a land that once seemed unfamiliar become a place you call your own?

In just five weeks, Tenwek Hospital was beginning to feel like home. The early morning breakfast of brown toast and papaya, the visits with patients before surgery, the daily greetings from Bob Wesche, Marty Graber, David Stevens, Dick Morse—we were family. Yet we would not be together much longer, because in six days I would be leaving. As I operated in a modern surgical ward back in California, assisted by an expert, trained staff, using the world's most advanced medical equipment, my Tenwek colleagues would be trying to use every last inch of suture. These were real missionary doctors, barraged by human needs, often lacking the most basic medicine and supplies. They worked at all hours, treating whatever disease or accident was put in front of them. Tenwek Hospital was the end of the line for the people in that part of the world. These doctors and nurses I worked alongside and came to admire were the last best hope a sick person had to become well again. The past six weeks had been some of the most demanding, draining, and satisfying medicine I had ever known. And it was all going by too fast.

Sylvia and I knew we had just barely peeked through the door of the Kipsigis culture. Yet, through this sliver of opportunity, I had peeked in on missionary medicine and Kipsigis culture, and met the one patient who made the two worlds one. But now the door was closing fast. Time was running out on the work and we both knew it.

With less than seventy-two hours to go, we had one more thing to do. "What are we going to do about visiting Stanley?" Elizabeth asked. "We did say were going to visit him in his hut," Robert answered. Nothing more needed to be said. Final plans were being made. Suitcases had to be packed. Promises had to be kept.

That Sunday after church services, Marty and Ann Graber stood outside the combi-van that would take the seven of us to Stanley's hut at Lelaitich. Marty approached me. "Mel, I've just gotten word that Stanley has been experiencing more pain." This was strange. How could Marty know? I knew Stanley didn't have a telephone, and his hut was twenty miles from Tenwek.

"How did you find this out, Marty?"

"Bush telegraph," Marty said, laughing. "With all the patients and hospital workers who come and go, somehow the word gets passed around. It's possible to send out a request for information and have a response come back almost the same day."

The road to Stanley's hut was rough and muddy. It had rained the night before. Inside, my anticipation began to cloud over. I tried to imagine what Stanley looked like in the four weeks since he'd left Tenwek. How much had the cancer eaten into his spine? Would he be wearing the artificial leg we had brought him from America? What would I feel as we visited and said goodbye for what would probably be the final time?

Green rolling hills turned to sparse, rocky earth. A turn came, and we were off the road, heading toward grassy plains I had visited before. This land wasn't what I expected at all. Instead of barren desert, Stanley's world looked like Kansas pastures. We pulled up to three mud huts, two with conical straw roofs, another with a sheet metal covering to shield the sun.

Outside the window, a group of about twenty-five people were gathered by the huts. The van stopped. As I got out of the vehicle, an elderly lady started toward us. As she came closer, I could see her smile. She was Stanley's mother, someone said. Though I couldn't make sense of her Kipsigis greeting, I understood her language of hospitality. She reached out her hands, wet with the precious water she must have carried from the river two miles away.

I said to Ann Graber, "Please tell Mrs. Cheborge that we are very pleased to meet her and that we are happy to be here to visit." My words were repeated in native Kipsigis and brought a broader smile to her face. Her obvious, quiet warmth was a language I could understand.

Then I saw Annah. "Welcome," she said. Her words were quiet and respectful. "We have waited for you." In seconds, we were surrounded by people wanting to shake our hands. For a moment I was back on the grass air strip at Bomet, enveloped again by an eerie, almost complete silence.

And then I saw Stanley.

He was lying on a pad on the ground in the center of where the Kipsigis had been sitting. "Oh, Dr. Graber, Dr. Cheatham, you have come to visit my home." Right away I knew we were part of something more than a house visit. I did not know yet what our presence meant to this man and all the others whose nameless faces puzzled me.

"Who are all of these people?" I asked Marty quietly.

"Relatives and friends of Stanley's," he answered.

It was an impressive but not uncommon sight. Patients who came to Tenwek were almost never alone. They were accompanied by people who loved them, who stayed by their bedsides, sometimes even through the night. That same commitment was now present with Stanley in the friends and family who stood by him at his home. Without any kind of prompting, the silent mass of Kipsigis moved to their designated places. People began to take their seats around Stanley. Sylvia and I, along with the Grabers, were given seats of honor next to where Stanley lay. Michael, Elizabeth, and Robert sat on cowhide laid out on the ground.

The setting was almost complete. I looked up and saw a man of obvious authority accompany Stanley's mother to the two remaining seats. He was Arap Cheborge, Stanley's father, the one I had only heard about but had not met. Stanley explained that these were his family and friends who had come to spend time with him. Then, the silence became almost total.

Mr. Cheborge stood up. He walked over to me, extended his right hand, and clasped my hand between both of his. They were rough, powerful hands, seasoned by years of hard work, and they made mine seem pale and insignificant by comparison. He cradled my hand in his and wouldn't let go. Then, in a loud, clear voice, he began to speak. It did not matter that I couldn't make sense of a single word. I knew every Kipsigis was listening to this powerful man whose words seemed uncommonly bold for someone of his tribe.

Then, as quickly as he began speaking, he stopped and abruptly walked away. I could see heads nod and smiles appear on the faces of the senior tribal members who had been granted the right of offering or denying approval. Who was this man whose words shook with emotion over his favorite son who now lay helpless?

"I will tell you what he meant," said Stanley. With others listening in, Arap Cheborge's Kipsigis suddenly became crisp English. "Dr. Cheatham, I thank God for bringing all of you to help care for the sick at Tenwek. I thank the Lord for the hands of the surgeon, the hands that operated on my son.

"Stanley is my son, and I have asked God to heal him. I know that God has a son, and His name is Jesus. For this reason, I speak now to God knowing that since He has this Son, He will understand the great love I have for my son. I will wait for God to heal Stanley and relieve him of his pain, so that he might live."

Now I understood this was a loving father's plea for help. Arap Cheborge and I sat separated by several thousand years of history, and by language—neither of us could understand the other's speech. Stanley had shortened the distance between our worlds from 10,000 miles to a few words. I had talked with scores of Kipsigis in my brief six weeks at Tenwek. All spoke their native Kipsigis. Some spoke English, quietly. But only Stanley had the capacity to understand both languages, translate both, and in so doing allow me to live in two cultures at once. Without an interpreter, I remained a foreign visitor, giving and receiving silent stares in a strange, still-distant world. With Stanley I had a sound track to match the moving picture I was a part of.

When Arap Cheborge had finished, Stanley translated his mother's warm welcome to us. Then everyone became quiet. Stanley took hold of the silence. "This is the place of my birth," he said to me. "This is the place of my life before going to the school at Tenwek. The place where I broke my leg is not far away. It is good that I have now been able to return to my home, my family, my friends of this tribe, and to my roots. This is where I should be to experience this difficulty in my life."

Stanley was using what little strength he had to find the words that mattered most.

"The Lord, in whom I have placed my complete trust, is with me always, no matter where I might be. I know that He is with me here in this place, and that He will bring healing to my body. There is much for me to do, and I must be well enough to continue with those things which God has laid before me to do."

I knew Stanley believed every word he was saying. Even as his body betrayed him, and the level of pain was now more than most people could endure, Stanley's faith had not moved an inch. Outwardly, however, this was not the same person I had known. In the four weeks since he had left Tenwek, Stanley had obviously lost weight. His face was drawn. He was now too weak to move. Not once did he shift from his reclining position. He supported himself on one elbow or the other.

Marty leaned down in front of Stanley. "How much pain have you been feeling?" he asked.

"I have experienced much pain," Stanley said. "But I am prepared to deal with it as I must." How much longer Stanley had to live, I couldn't tell. But I knew the time was short. Tenwek Hospital and its doctors and nurses had given Stanley about all they could offer medically. But regardless of what lay ahead, Tenwek had offered Stanley something more. It had given him people like David Kilel and Ernie Steury through whom Stanley had heard the promise of eternal life in Jesus Christ. And because he had accepted Him, Stanley Cheborge knew he would live beyond his earthly life.

I looked at my watch. Our time was just about up. I looked over at Marty, and I could see he and Ann were getting ready to leave. Afternoon was fading, running away with the remaining daylight we needed for our drive back to Tenwek.

I knelt down next to Stanley and I looked into his deep, brown eyes. I saw the once-far-away Kenyan who needed the new artificial leg. I saw the patient so ready to laugh and so unafraid to cry when he finally stood up on his artificial limb and knew the pain was too great. I saw a common man of uncommon conviction. I saw a children's Sunday school teacher who walked seven miles on one leg, steadied only by a stick. I looked past the pain and saw a much younger man who used to run with the wind, confident he could have anything he wanted in life, until cancer cut his steps short. Now, he was lying on the ground, a few footsteps from the place where he was born twenty-six years before, nearly as helpless as a baby.

I reached out and took his hand.

"Thank you for operating on my spine, Dr. Cheatham, and for bringing me the new leg from America. After the Lord has healed my body, I will wear that leg as I continue the work He has called me to do."

"It has been my pleasure to help you, Stanley, and to become your friend. We will have you in our prayers as we return to America. Goodbye and God bless you."

With that, I turned with Sylvia, Michael, Elizabeth, and Robert, and walked toward the van. As we started to climb into the vehicle, I noticed Mrs. Cheborge and Annah, holding a chicken, a final gift.

"Thank you," Sylvia said, as she took the chicken and laid it on the floor between the seats. Its legs were tied together so it could not run away. I looked out the window and there were at least twenty people surrounding the vehicle, all waving as we drove away. In the distance I could see Stanley, lying on the ground. Even with its legs tied, the chicken enjoyed more freedom than Stanley. He would never walk or run again.

During the drive back to Tenwek, the thoughts of my friend stretched out for the next two hours. After seeing Stanley the scenery looked different. No matter what the terrain, whether scrub brush or green fields filed by my window, I noticed the people. A barefoot mother carried a load of wood on her back, a crying child wrapped in a cloth slung over her shoulder. A hunched over man struggled with each step, alone. Where were they all going? Where had they come from? How many more Stanley's, who need medicine or a life-saving operation, had been left back home? If these people had any hope of being well again, if they had strength for the journey and a family to go with, I knew Tenwek Hospital was waiting to take them in.

It was dark when we drove up the road to the hospital. Our departure was less than twelve hours away. When we walked into our guest quarters, we began packing immediately. As I folded my clothes and put them in the suitcase, I found a folded piece of paper. It was the list Michael and I had put together, the take-it-for-granted supplies most U.S. hospitals stock in abundance—surgical instruments, towels, sutures, blood pressure/pulse monitors, a suction machine that works. Tenwek needed all these things. I knew we could get every one of them in the U.S. and ship them back here. It would be the most helpful contribution I could make.

It was 10:00 p.m., and the suitcases were almost full. Michael and I walked up to the hospital to collect my bag of neurosurgical instruments. As we approached the compound I noticed the lights were on in one of the operating theaters. I looked through the window and saw Bob Wesche and Carlos Somoza engaged in surgery. I knew by word-of-mouth the patient was an elderly man with a bowel obstruction. Without surgery, he would worsen, experience overwhelming infection, and die. They were having to do the surgery under local anesthesia. Under these circumstances, the risk he might die on the table was very high. Scores of patients would face similar surgeries in the U.S. the next day with little such risk. This man's survival depended, in part, on whatever anesthesia could be found on Tenwek's shelf. It didn't seem right.

And what could I do? My time was up. The next day I'd be flying back home to a modern hospital with the very latest in medical technology and almost every conceivable kind of medication and supplies. I knew I had given something that was intense and valued by Tenwek's patients and staff. However, my work was only a ripple in the ocean of need confronted daily by the doctors who remained. Tomorrow, Bob and Carlos would be wishing they could get their hands on the most common spinal anesthetic, some additional suture, antibiotics, and a few more surgical clamps.

The demands facing them never stopped. And yet, on the morning we left Tenwek, they were still giving to us. It was a sight I'll never forget: All five members of our family stood on the grass outside the Steury home, surrounded by the hospital's entire missionary staff. Suddenly, I was hit by the fact that my picture of Tenwek was not a mere snapshot stuck in my mind; the past six weeks had grown into a tapestry that had woven together every member of the Cheatham family. For Bob, Tenwek, like so many other previous family journeys abroad, had eclipsed any college classroom experience. "Definitely, the hardest I have ever worked," he would say when I asked him to describe his four-day-a-week project of putting Tenwek's inventory on computer. He even found a new appreciation for emergency medicine when a swarm of killer bees attacked him one day on the compound and caused his arm to double in size. The swelling eventually went down, but my youngest son's awareness of the Third World and the commitment of Tenwek's missionaries had been enlarged permanently.

Elizabeth had written a new deputation brochure to help missionaries tell their stories while on furlough. Thanks to her interviewing skills, Stanley's voice was now on tape. For Elizabeth, Africa would no longer be merely a place on a map or a headline in the newspaper. She had invested too much of herself to forget a one-legged patient and the place he called home.

Michael, my oldest son, hated leaving Tenwek. For one who had just finished his first year at Vanderbilt School of Medicine in Nashville, this had been a perfect training ground. He was my assistant in surgery, and the more time he spent in the operating theater, the more he came to see that general surgery was his calling and that working long-term at a place like Tenwek was no longer a question of If? but When?

Sylvia had yet to stand across the operating table from me, but I knew the time would come on a return trip that was now just a matter of time.

Woven into the tapestry of the last six weeks was the common thread of warmth from each hospital staff person who had stopped what he or she was doing and had walked down the road to say goodbye. The feeling of love and friendship was overwhelming. I wanted to shake every hand and hug every person, but time wasn't willing to wait. We had to go.

I climbed into the van that would take us to the grass landing strip at Kericho fifty miles away. There, a Cessna from African Inland Mission would fly us on to Nairobi. I shook Bob Wesche's hand. "If Stanley develops too much pain, I'll come back and do an operation, called a cordotomy, in which I'll partially sever his spinal cord so that he doesn't feel pain below his rib cage."

"What are you saying?" I thought to myself. I was offering to fly 10,000 miles back to Kenya, perform a two-hour operation, then turn around and fly 10,000 miles back to California. It was both outrageous and totally do-able. I knew there weren't any other neurosurgeons coming to Tenwek. If Stanley needed such surgery, I was the only one who could do it. I could leave Tenwek Hospital, but I couldn't distance myself from the reality.

As our plane flew over the Maasai Mara later that morning, I knew that in one of those scattered mud huts two thousand feet below, Stanley Cheborge lay dying from cancer.

Flying through ten time zones didn't take me any farther from the truth. Thirty hours later I was flying over my village of ten million people. From the air, I looked through the hazy brown clouds and could see the town of Ventura, resting on the coast. Once on the ground, the freeways ran fast, all the way to the Seaward off-ramp that led to our house. It looked the same as the day we left.

So did the hospital, my office, and the partners I returned to the following day. The schedule was as full as ever. My world didn't look all that different, except I saw some familiar sights for the first time.

In the operating room I was surrounded by million-dollar anesthesia equipment that Tenwek would never have. There were yards of suture that someone like Bob Wesche could use to sew up a cut hand or an infected leg. Why couldn't the medical people I know donate surgical instruments and supplies to help patients half a world away? I asked Keith Hanstad, a surgical equipment representative, for help. Within two weeks, a crate of instruments was headed for Tenwek.

At the hospital in Ventura, I saw foam rubber "egg crate" mattresses on patients' beds. Stanley needed one of those. How many more like him in impoverished corners of the globe would go to sleep that night on a hard dirt floor? Six weeks before, I wouldn't have asked the question. Now, I couldn't walk away from the needs I had seen and touched through one person. Without trying, Stanley Cheborge had become my handshake, my dialogue, my relationship with the Third World.

Six weeks went by. I heard nothing about his condition, until one evening when I came home from work, I opened an aerogram from Marty and Ann Graber. My eyes jumped to the second paragraph.

"Our family went to visit Stanley and Annah Cheborge this afternoon. We found him, again, outside his house on a pad. He is a bit thinner and seemed a bit anxious, but he was trying to keep his spirits up."

I put the letter down and tried to envision him lying on the ground in southwestern Kenya, with cancer eating away at his spine, with little medical care.

"Stanley said he thinks he is feeling a little better after being treated by bush medicine. He seemed to be trying to show faith, but our observation of him did not match everything he was saying."

Marty explained that Stanley had seen a bush medicine doctor. Instead of being taken to Kenyatta Hospital in Nairobi, where I had arranged for radiation therapy on his spine, Stanley turned to the herbal concoctions of a witch doctor.

To a physician and just about anyone who has grown up relying on the medical profession, this was like choosing folklore over a hospital. I didn't pretend to know Stanley's culture and its ways. I could only assume he must have been under pressure to receive tribal medicine.

Then, six weeks later, another letter came. This one was from Bob and Dora Wesche. In the lower left hand corner of their newsletter I saw the one-word headline: "Puzzling." Underneath were these few telling sentences:

"Two outstanding men have both been struck with recurrent bone cancer. Weston Kirui, age twenty, died this spring, and Stanley Cheborge, twenty-eight, has been in the hospital five weeks now and was not expected to live even this long. Stanley is a Bible school graduate. Why God elects to take choice young men, with such potential for Christian service, and take them home early, is puzzling to us. God does all things well.

Please pray for both of their families, especially Annah, who will soon give birth to their baby."

The news of their child brought only some comfort, because a few days later, another letter arrived. This one was from David Stevens:

"You would be interested to know that Stanley Cheborge is now home. Being back with his family has done much for his mood, but it is difficult to know how much longer he will hang on, especially without medical care."

October arrived, three months after we had seen Stanley Cheborge stretched out on the ground in front of his family's hut. I wondered if he even resembled the person I had known.

As the days and weeks passed, the pain in Stanley's lower back and leg had grown worse. He was an invalid, dependent on his family to feed him, give him drinks of water, and monitor the mushrooming tumor that had opened up and was beginning to fester and drain. There was more bush medicine. Tribesmen applied a mud pack to encase the mass, but the tumor only erupted through the mud. The pain, infection, and bleeding engulfed Stanley's body, and shook his family. Only one choice was left—to take him back to Tenwek and see if any help were possible.

In the back of a matatu, Stanley endured the bumpy, twisting two hour drive to the hospital. Immediately, once inside the gate, the call went out: "Please ask Dr. Wesche to come. Tell him Stanley Cheborge is here."

Stanley was carried into one of the small hospital rooms. Moments later, Dr. Wesche was in the room. The person he saw bore no resemblance to the one-legged man whose smile and spirit for life had been contagious. Dr. Wesche looked at the tumor. It was now the size of two clenched fists, protruding from Stanley's lower back. "We need four pints of blood," Dr. Wesche ordered.

The next few days groaned by. Stanley received eighteen blood transfusions. Each one pumped new life into him. Strength came back, and it left him just as quickly. The bleeding continued. It drained him of energy. It drained him of life. The cancer had almost completed its assignment of robbing Stanley of his dignity. It could not, however, take away what he knew inside to be true.

"I feel that I will live, but if I do not, then I know I will go to heaven," he said, now forced to lie on his stomach by the awkward, engulfing presence of the tumor on his back.

Stanley was in a race against time. His wife's pregnancy had dwindled from a number of days to a matter of hours. Stanley knew it. "I wait anxiously for the birth of our child," he said. His once booming voice had now been silenced to a strained whisper. "A son will carry on for me and will keep the fire burning." The doctors at Tenwek who had known Stanley, who had seen him walk in leaps with his crutch, and who had watched him stumble under cancer's cruel weight, now kept him alive with blood transfusions to fulfill his wish; he wanted to see his son born.

The hours crawled on. The day came. October 5, 1986. Grace Cherotich Cheborge entered the world. A girl. A daughter, who would be the only heir of Stanley Cheborge.

Ann Graber leaned down and whispered the news in Stanley's ear. For a moment, he was stunned. Shock turned to disappointment. Then a wide grin crept across his face. "I am thankful to God for the blessing of this child, who has been given to us. We will raise her to know and love the Lord, even as we have done. Yes, I give thanks."

The smile beamed wider when Grace was placed into his arms for the first time. There would be no male heir. But for Stanley and Annah there could be no disappointment in one precious new life. But even in this joy, another struggle was being born. Kipsigis tribal tradition called for one of Stanley's brothers to assume the role as husband to Annah after she became a widow. In this way, the seed could be passed on, to "keep the fire burning" for the tribe.

"I cannot do it! I will not do it, Stanley!" Annah bent down to her husband's face in a rare moment when other family members were gone. "We both know that if I marry one of your brothers, I would violate my beliefs as a Christian."

Stanley listened. "I know this," he said, "but others in our family do not see things the same way. I do not want to think of the problems ahead. . . ."

The menacing tumor was fully out of control. But despite the pain, it was still a small open sore compared to the huge anxiety he felt for Annah, his baby daughter, and what lay ahead of them. A few mornings later, he asked his family, Dr. Wesche and a handful of Tenwek's staff to come to his room.

When they were all gathered around his bed, Stanley reached down inside himself to find the strength to speak.

"There is something I need you to hear. But most of all this is for my wife, Annah. It is about a decision she must make. When the time has come for me to die, she needs to decide on one of three choices: The first is she can marry the person of her choosing. The second is she can stay with the family with one of my brothers as her husband. The third choice is she can be free to do whatever she wants to."

There was silence in the room. Stanley's brothers couldn't approve of the choice Stanley was giving Annah. Didn't he know that option two was the only acceptable way under Kipsigis tradition? As strongly as they felt about this, neither said a word to their dying brother.

By giving his wife the option not to marry one of his brothers, Stanley stood Kipsigis culture on its head. Stanley was giving Annah the unheard of freedom to choose her own future.

By doing so he knew he risked losing the love and acceptance of the one person in life he wanted most to please, his father. And he did this knowing his father would likely never understand. Every person surrounding his withered frame saw clearly that Stanley was choosing to put God before the expectations of his tribe.

For many it was unheard of. How could someone make such a decision, unless he knew he could trust this God of the Bible with his life?

The blood transfusions gave Stanley enough strength so he could be taken to his hut near the Maasai border. The days and nights that followed brought more humiliation. In the morning his family moved Stanley outside the hut where he could lie in the shade of a tree. At night he lay on the hard mud floor of the hut on a thin, foam rubber pad.

He was lying on his side when Bob Wesche and David Kilel, Stanley's long-time friend and spiritual mentor, came to visit him.

"On the ground we saw this once-strong, muscular athlete who was now an emaciated mass of skin and bone," Bob said. With a weakened grip, Stanley reached out to accept the hand of his surgeon and friend.

"My friends, you have come to visit me. Your presence gives me strength."

The three sat together outside the hut until the long shadows fell over Stanley. They bowed their heads in silence. Then David Kilel prayed, "Our God, you know us better than we know ourselves. You know Stanley, and it is he we pray for right now. God, in your mercy, we ask that you show us a sign that might indicate to us whether Stanley is to die or be healed of his cancer. Amen."

The three raised their heads and opened their eyes. David's words were still hanging in the air when Stanley's tumor split open. Bright red blood streamed down both sides of his back. Bob Wesche looked at Stanley as he started to speak.

"Dr. Wesche, can you not relieve my terrible pain?" Stanley said looking up with wide, pleading eyes.

"The Pethedine will help, but there is nothing we can give to completely relieve the pain."

Stanley woke up at dawn. Now lapsing in and out of coma, his words were few. "Last night I would have died," he told two visiting friends, Caleb Langot and John Koech. "But God saved me to live again today. I have suffered greatly and I have grown as a Christian. The rest of my life I am giving to the Lord."

When Stanley opened his eyes, there was his father. Arap Cheborge had sat at his bedside throughout the night. Stanley saw the wrinkled lines and the damp eyes of the elderly man. "Father, I am assured this disease, this cancer, is going to take my life. I now know that I am about to die." Stanley caught his breath and glanced down.

"Father, I will not be able to care for you and my mother in your old age. I have failed my responsibility."

As Arap Cheborge took the cold, near-lifeless hand, he remembered Stanley as a little boy, who was now a dying man.

"All that could be done to help you has been done. There is nothing else we can do, my son," he said, his voice trembling. He was not alone in his grief. Next to Stanley, his wife looked on. In her arms was their new child. It was Annah who longed to cry. Kipsigis tradition, however, said she could not; so long as Stanley still lived, crying might bring death more quickly.

But tradition was painfully moot. Stanley's breathing slowed. By now, his chest barely moved. Arap Cheborge held onto his son's hand. Without knowing that his son had finally stopped breathing, he sat alone, afraid to express his deepest loss, still hiding a thousand tears his son would never see.

NINE

"Dear Mel and Sylvia, . . ."

I didn't get more than two sentences past the greeting when Bob Wesche's news stopped me. I put down the aerogram, and my world became unusually quiet.

My friend was gone. He'd lived just long enough to hold his baby daughter in his arms. In the Cheborge hut I could see a father weeping and a baby sleeping in the arms of her widowed mother. And I could see Stanley, a son, a husband, and a father, running up the path to a new home shining in heaven's light.

Something stirred inside. I looked at Sylvia and we both knew what was about to happen. It had been growing inside us for weeks. Now, the news of Stanley's death turned our desires into virtual certainty. Six weeks at Tenwek had changed us. We could leave the compound, but not the people, nor the lines of desperate faces belonging to families who needed help, medicine, surgery, and rest. They needed a place at the end of the road that would take them in, where their bones could heal and their bodies could mend. That was Tenwek, and for however full our time had been there, six weeks hadn't been long enough.

And now this news about Stanley. His life, and now his death, brought home the world of faith and hope and suffering that was Tenwek. Judy Streamer heard the story. A surgical nurse at Ventura Community Hospital, she saw our slides of Kipsigis patients, sitting three to a bed, and visiting American nurses who worked in hospitals just like she did. We told her the stories, recounted our footsteps, relived the hours.

"When you go back, I'd like to go," she said. "What do they need at the hospital?" We told her they needed spinal anesthesia. For the next weeks and months, Judy collected vials of Pontocaine from single use anesthesia trays that would otherwise have been discarded. We told her of our plans to return. She began to look at her calendar. Kenya started to look a lot closer, for all of us.

I told Dr. Nellie Mac, an anesthesiology colleague of mine in Ventura, about Tenwek. "You know, Nellie, it sure would be good to have an anesthesiologist at Tenwek."

"When do you plan on going?"

April seemed like a possibility. We would go for three weeks. I arranged it with my associates at work. I knew what waited for us. The flight would be long, the work hard and intense. It started as soon as we arrived at Tenwek and began unpacking the six duffel bags and two footlockers filled with equipment and supplies. Bob Wesche and Steven Mabutu watched as we carried our things into the storage area between the two operating rooms. It must have been a pleasant sight for them as we brought in boxes of suture, new surgical towels, antibiotics, and a cautery machine used to control bleeding during operations. Nellie, Judy, Sylvia, and I dressed in our green surgical scrub suits. Then we each grabbed all the equipment and supplies we could carry and headed up the hill to the hospital. I had walked this path before. Nothing seemed to have changed in the nine months since our first arrival. Large numbers of patients still waited in clusters to be seen. We walked into the operating theater, and there was Bob Wesche busy doing a skin graft on a child with a burn.

"Bob?" I said. "We have some new, sharp Brown dermatone blades for you to use in taking the skin for grafting."

"Great," he responded. "You've arrived with them just in time. It's been pretty tough trying to harvest skin, only ten-one-thousandth of an inch thick, with dull dermatone blades." Bob was smiling. Christmas had come eight months early.

Nellie, Judy, and I toured the pediatrics wards, then saw the men and women patients. On the way back to the operating theater, we passed the room where I had visited Stanley. My thoughts flashed back to this unique, young man, all that I had learned from him, and the way he had lived his life. He was gone now, but not his memory, nor the inspiration he had brought to others.

Everything about Tenwek Hospital seemed very familiar. Until we were greeted by someone we had never seen before. His gray, nearly white hair, belied his age and his boundless energy.

"Mel Cheatham, it's good to meet you."

"It's good to meet you, Ernie," I said.

"I'm glad our paths crossed," he replied. "When you and Sylvia were here before, Sue and I were back in Indiana on furlough. We'd like the four of you to come to our house for lunch."

"We'd be most happy to join you."

I'll never forget my initial meeting with this man. He had the silent charisma of someone who's lived his life as a servant of Jesus Christ. There was nothing loud, or showy, or boastful about him, just the genuineness of someone who places the needs and well-being of others first.

Ernie stood about five feet, ten inches tall. Yet I soon learned that inside this slight frame was a workhorse. As we walked together down the hill, he told us about his efforts as executive officer, and how he spent most of his time administering. He described the endless meetings with the National staff, government officials, and communications with World Gospel Mission back in the U.S.

"It's a real joy sometimes just to be able to go to the operating theater and do what I've been trained to do—operate on someone who is sick and in need. Unfortunately, such opportunities don't come along often enough these days."

Sue Steury greeted us at the door. Warm, friendly, and charming, it was obvious that she was the other half of the Steury partnership. This remarkable couple had given the prime of their adult lives to this cause of medical missionary service called Tenwek Hospital.

We talked over helpings of Indian curry and rice. And in between bites I began to learn more about this much-talked about man, where he had come from, how he had wound up at Tenwek. And why he and his wife had stayed for almost thirty years.

He had gone to Asbury College in Wilmore, Kentucky, with plans to become an evangelistic missionary. "I wanted to do church planting work, until my roommate planted the seed of an idea that God germinated into a real opportunity—applying for medical school and training to become a medical missionary. So I changed my major to pre-med and applied to the University of Indiana School of Medicine.

"My interview for medical school consisted of responding to three questions: Why did I want to become a medical doctor? Was I afraid that if I went into the jungle as a medical missionary the natives might put me in a pot of boiling water? Did I expect to see any tigers in Africa?

"Lord," I prayed, "why didn't the interviewers take me any more seriously than that? I was sure they weren't going to let me in. Three weeks later, a letter came saying I had been accepted."

Ernie revealed that just one minor item might have kept him from fulfilling his desire to become a medical missionary in Africa.

"I had no money! I talked with Dr. George Warner, the president of World Gospel Mission, about the possibility of financial support. A few days later the phone rang. Dr. Warner was calling to tell me that a check for $10,000 had just been received from a person who wanted to sponsor a medical student who would be willing to become a medical missionary."

In May 1959 Ernie and Sue Steury arrived in Kericho for six months of language school at Kenya Highlands Bible College. Then they were assigned to a thirty-two-bed dispensary called Tenwek Hospital.

He explained that technically he was a family practitioner. However, since Tenwek was the only source of medical care for people with no other hospital, Ernie had to deal with every disease, every unexplained pain that came in the door. As he told of these experiences and the lack of medication, staff, and other physicians to consult, it occurred to me that when it came to medical expertise, Ernie Steury lacked nothing. He was a real doctor. I thought my six weeks at Tenwek had been demanding. But this man was teaching me the real definition of "demanding."

"Our acceptance by the Kipsigis went slow. Still the work load was almost overpowering. I can't count the times I would work all day, all that night, and then into the next day and night and the *next* day as well. I would be physically and emotionally spent. I would be so tired, there was no way I could do any more work.

"I would drop into bed, and some time later there would be a tap on the window. And I would know I was needed again."

I pictured this man who at times was up for seventy-two hours straight, a lone surgeon with no associates, no clinic, no other hospital to fall back on, walking down a dark path by the light of a flashlight, to perform another surgery. How was it possible?

"The Lord just answered my prayers for the strength required, and I did what I had to do."

Listening to Ernie, I thought about myself. What would I do if the patient, or the urgent problem, pushed me to my limit? When would I face another operation that was as medically demanding as Stanley Cheborge's? Or greater?

One day I met Dr. Dick Morse. He was the second physician to come to Tenwek, joining the staff in Ernie's tenth year. Dick was a hard worker, often treating sick children until 11:00 at night. One morning, he asked me to see a little twelve-year-old Kipsigis girl.

"I think she might have a brain tumor, Mel. She's had terrible headaches and vomiting. Can you look at her right away?"

Five minutes later, I saw her lying on a bed in agony. She tried not to move from her curled-up position, because any movement simply made the headache worse. Whenever she tried to stand or walk, she would fall. I looked inside her eyes and I could see papilloedema—swelling of the optic nerves due to high pressure in the brain. I suspected a brain tumor in the fourth ventricle at the base of the brain, and decided to do a shunt operation to at least relieve the pressure inside her head.

First, I drilled a one-half inch hole through her skull. Then, I inserted a silastic tube inside her brain, and ran it down behind the ear, under her skin, down the neck to the chest. Then I inserted the other end into the abdominal cavity surrounded by her intestine. As I drilled the opening in her head, I injected a small amount of air into the enlarged fluid space inside her brain, then lifted her through a backward somersault, and took an X-ray of her head.

The technique of doing a "bubble ventriculogram" such as this was something Dr. Williamson and Dr. Brackett had taught me in my neurosurgical training. This was years before the technological breakthrough of CT and MRI scanning. That morning at Tenwek, lacking such superior equipment, I was standing back in the 1950s, practicing the very techniques my two mentors had taught me. The student had become the physician.

Once she was somersaulted backwards 180 degrees, I took an X-ray of her head. The film showed just what I had suspected: air outlined a tumor in the midline of the posterior part of her brain. This little girl was going to die if I didn't operate.

The clock was running. By inserting the shunt, the intense pressure in her brain decreased. She had relief from the headache and vomiting. Standing next to me was Dr. Nellie Mac. Without an anesthesiologist like her to work with, operating on a brain tumor would have been completely out of the question. With Nellie there, it was a reasonable possibility.

Nellie, Judy, and I talked. We decided to operate on the child's brain. Probably the procedure would be the first brain tumor operation ever done at Tenwek. But immediately, there were problems. There was no oxygen available. A four-hour surgery could take two tanks of oxygen. We told David Stevens of the need.

"Is oxygen available in these outer parts?" I asked him.

"Yes," he said. Then he asked me, "Could surgery wait another day until the oxygen is brought back?" I told him it could. After I described what had to be done, he said, "I'll see what I can do." Then he jumped into a van and headed for Kericho, a town fifty miles away by dirt road. Five hours later David was back. He walked into the operating theater room where Nellie, Judy, and I were working. "I went to a small government hospital. This is all I could get," he said as two of the Nationals carried in a single oxygen tank. It was half of what we really needed to safely do the surgery, and we knew there wouldn't be any more. However, we needed more than oxygen.

Early the next morning I found Nellie working on Tenwek's old anesthesia machine. The frustration on her face told me she had been there more than a few minutes. "I can't get it to work well enough to do brain surgery anesthesia," she said. Driving another fifty miles and back for a new anesthesia machine was not an option. Then we had an idea.

We called "Uncle" Charlie Snyder and asked him if he would come and help us. Charlie Snyder was a big man. At six feet, three inches, he had powerful muscles, a full head of white, wavy hair, and a long, white handle-bar mustache. He paid all of his own expenses to fly to Tenwek from his home in Toronto for one to two months just to "help out." And he did this not just once, but two or three times a year. Uncle Charlie had the gift of being able to fix almost anything. Within an hour after arriving in the operating theater, he had the anesthesia machine running.

"It will work, Mel, but it won't flush additional oxygen into the system if we need it," Nellie said. This was not good. I stepped back and saw how much we were missing. There was no operating microscope. The anesthesia machine was marginal at best. We had only one tank of oxygen and if this ran out before the operation was completed, the little girl would have only room air to breathe. Then there was a whole host of neurosurgical instruments we just plain didn't have. Things so basic and now so lacking, such as a frame for positioning this little girl, and holding her head still during surgery.

I looked over at Nellie. "Let's go outside and talk." We left the operating theater and walked down the hallway. "Are we making a big mistake by trying to do this surgery under these conditions?" A long silence passed. Then she looked at me and said, "We've prepared as best we can. We have prayed about it. If we don't go ahead, she's going to die. Let's go for it."

We walked back inside the operating theater. It was now late morning, two days after I had first seen this little girl. I realized she needed far more than equipment. She needed a surgeon's steady hand, a skilled team, and God to guide us.

Her head was positioned in a halo vest donated by a patient from Ventura who had worn it for a broken neck. In place of an operating microscope, we used a set of ear, nose, and throat magnifying binoculars that had been left at Tenwek by Dr. Mike McGee from Oklahoma City.

Four hours later, we put the last stitch in the skin. The operation was finished. We still had oxygen left. The anesthesia machine had worked. I saw a wide grin on the face of this girl when she woke up. How was it logically possible to have successfully operated in the deepest corners of her brain when every shortcoming we faced said it couldn't be done?

God's intervention is not logical. It is only inexplicably real, awesome, and true. And the reason I know is because, when everything around Nellie and me was literally falling apart, we prayed and asked God to help us. The smile of a twelve-year-old girl waking up after surgery, the way she walked out of Tenwek and resumed a healthy life only days later, was the answer to our prayers. Her healing was a reminder of how I had increasingly come to depend upon God to help me deal with broken anesthesia machines and some big questions I had begun to face.

Tenwek didn't really need a neurosurgeon with my specialist training. Most patients required general surgery—"bread and butter" operations like appendectomies, removal of a bowel obstruction, or C-sections. This was where Ernie Steury and Bob Wesche shined, and because of them my Tenwek experience was never the same. In the weeks we operated together, I watched, I listened, I learned how to be a better general surgeon. I felt my comfort level and efficiency increase because of Ernie and Bob. By the time we left for home at the end of April, Ernie Steury and Bob Wesche were more than colleagues; they had become Christian friends I cared for very much. I knew what their presence, or absence, would mean to each other. Come September, Bob would return to the U.S. on furlough. Without a general surgeon to replace him, the burden of the surgery and care for as many as sixty surgical patients a week would fall solely on Ernie. Before I left Tenwek I told him, "Ernie, maybe I can come back in September and help out." Before the day was over I was thankful that I was still breathing and able to think about returning.

The morning of our departure greeted Nellie, Judy, Sylvia, and me with some unsettling news: the grass airstrip at Bomet was too short for the five-seat Cessna to lift off with all our baggage. Jim Straight, the pilot, had an idea. He would fly me and my bags to a landing strip at Narok, return to pick up the women at Tenwek, then come back for me and fly on to Nairobi.

We passed over vast stretches of zebra, gazelle, and wildebeests. The land was so desolate. I began to feel anxious, imagining myself standing alone with no other sign of human life. "I think we can save some time if we don't take you to Narok," Jim said, scouring the terrain outside the plane's wind-shield. My worst thoughts were coming true. As the plane touched down on a dusty strip of earth, I wondered what I would do when Jim left.

"I'll go for the others and be back to get you in about forty-five minutes," he said, handing me his large pilot binocu-lars and my 35 millimeter camera. Then he climbed back inside the cockpit, revved the engine, and taxied the plane around. With the engine roaring, the winged-creature lifted off, and within two minutes it was out of sight.

Now, there was dead silence. Except for a small curl of smoke coming from a mud hut in the distance, I was alone. I looked north through the binoculars. Something on the horizon was moving. It looked like three men.

Though they moved as specks, their shimmering figures started to grow. And so did my fear. "I am out here, totally alone," I said to myself. Closer and closer they walked, until by the time they were within shouting distance, my heart was beating like a drum. From the way they were dressed, I could tell the three men were Maasai.

"We think you have trouble," said one in broken English. "No, I don't have any trouble," I answered. The three were now moving into positions around me, one totally out of sight at my back. I had to remain cool.

"My friends and our airplane will be back to get me very soon." We stood there eye-balling each other. The hands on my watch must have stopped. Lord, protect me, I thought. I was the defenseless creature in the habitat I had marveled at earlier on safari. To these three, stalking strangers, I was either an interesting novelty or choice prey. Suddenly one of them pointed west and said, "The airplane, that one." I could see nothing but blue sky. The only sound was that of buffalo grass blowing in the breeze. Then I saw it. The airplane, my hope and safety, was a speck in the distance. The three men moved back and started to walk away, slowly. I marveled at the Maasai's sense of sight and sound; through their visit and peaceful exit, I knew I did not walk alone in uncharted deserts. I knew my prayers, however anxious they sounded, had been heard. I knew that, next to an African sunset, there was no more beautiful sight than a single-engine Cessna touching down on earth.

After another forty-five-minute flight to Nairobi, and twenty-four flying hours in a slightly more spacious 747, we were back home in Ventura. By July, no replacement was scheduled for Bob Wesche back at Tenwek. In California, it was summer and the heat was on. With one or more of my associates on vacation, my patient load was growing more and more demanding. I had to write Ernie: perhaps I should stay in Ventura and work. I could make a sizable financial contribution to help purchase new equipment or build critically needed missionary housing at Tenwek. I knew what Ernie's response would be. "Great, stay in California. Send the money and we'll manage the work here." When I opened his letter a few weeks later, it was worded somewhat differently: "We sure could use the amount of money you mentioned. But, we need you working here in September much more than we need the money. No general surgeon will be available until October. Our staffing problem is critical."

What a tragedy. To have people wait days to see a doctor who might lack the medicine to do anything, and to know that people in other countries might die because they had no Tenwek, all this hit home in Ernie's letter. I thought of Stanley and the ways he had overcome the tragedies and unfairness in his life. I remembered him describing the huge steps he learned to take by lunging forward using his crutch. How could he cover so much ground with so little? That was the paradox, and the beauty of the Kipsigis who had let me see into his world. The more Ernie's request underlined the needs at Tenwek, the more I knew that I was not being asked to make the convenient response of giving money, but the costlier sacrifice of giving myself to a part of the world that was now my other home.

Returning to Tenwek also carried a very real price tag.

On the last afternoon before Sylvia and I left for our third trip to Tenwek, my associates at work called a meeting to discuss my being gone so much. That afternoon I came away feeling totally tired and discouraged. As we flew to Africa, I faced a major decision: Because of increased time commitments, I either had to officially reduce my neurosurgical practice, or give up my current level of involvement with World Medical Mission. I knew the hectic pace of an extremely busy practice was not going to change, nor was my service to Tenwek, or wherever I was needed. Something had to give.

"What do you want to do, Mel?" Ed Wright was asking me that question again. It was now thirty-five years later and I had already lived my way into the answer. I wanted to return to the place where my eyes and heart had been opened to what I could give to hurting people as a Christian physician. I wanted to work alongside Ernie Steury and all the others who were laboring night and day. I wanted to invest in something that would live on after I died, knowing that I wasn't trying to further the mission of Mel Cheatham, but the life-giving, life-eternal work of Jesus Christ. That's why I couldn't turn my back on what little I could offer those who needed so much. That's why Sylvia and I decided to go back to Tenwek. This time I knew the needs would be great. However, I didn't expect them to be almost overwhelming.

I arrived at Tenwek feeling incredibly fatigued. For seven straight days and nights before we left Ventura for a post-graduate meeting on neurosurgery in Canada, I had been on call. This meant responding to round-the-clock emergencies and ongoing needs of patients of all three of my associates who decided to take that week as vacation. Tenwek was hurting. The hospital was critically low on missionary staff and supplies. I knew days before I walked onto the compound that the surgical cases would be backed up. I didn't have a moment to breathe. I had even less time to gown up in my surgical greens.

The good news was we had returned to Tenwek with a team. Amazingly, it had taken only two phone calls.

In June I called Dr. Bill Martin, an anesthesiologist, and his wife B.J. in Santa Maria, 100 miles up the California coast. I had gotten to know Bill when he worked in Ventura twenty years earlier.

"Bill, I've got a favor to ask."

"You name it, Mel."

"Bill, will you and B.J. go to Africa with Sylvia and me to help out a Christian mission hospital?"

"When?" he asked.

"September." There was a pause for about ten seconds. Here I was, asking a friend to fly 10,000 miles to Kenya, not for the thrill of enjoying a wild animal safari, but to work ten- and twelve-hour days in a hospital for three weeks. As the phone line remained silent, I could hear Bill processing all this in his mind. Would he do it?

There was no doubt in his decision. "Sure," he said. "I'll go, just as long as B.J. can go with me. We are a team."

It was the eleventh hour when I called Nora Caffrey, a Christian surgical nursing friend for twenty years. Nora is not more than five feet tall, but she stands tall in her own right. A native Filipino, she lived under Japanese occupation during World War II. She was no stranger to personal hardship. Besides being an excellent nurse she brought great spunk and energy into the operating room in Ventura. On the top of her surgical cap, she had embroidered a message to anyone who would look down on her:

X		O
	X	O
O		X

Why tall doctors like short scrub nurses?

A few weeks before we left, I called her. "Nora, I know this is short notice, but the hospital we're going to needs you. You will never see greater human need in one place than you will at Tenwek. You will never work harder or enjoy it more."

Nora said, "I'll go." Her decision meant even more when I realized Nora would not only lose three weeks of income, she would be paying all of her own expenses as well.

Bill and B.J. and Nora Caffrey brought community to Tenwek. The trip itself brought a sobering realization: For the next twenty-one days, I would be the lone surgeon in the only hospital equipped to care for a region of 300,000 people. Fortunately I had a partner to help me. While Bob Wesche was back in Michigan and Ernie Steury was at his desk plowing through paper work, I had company. My assistant had no formal medical credentials, yet she had remarkable perseverance that can't be learned in a laboratory or lecture hall. More than once at a natural impasse during surgery, I looked up and saw, standing across the table from me, Sylvia, my wife. She was so poised and alert, the woman who had been my partner for twenty-eight years. Gowned and gloved, she was my assistant and second pair of hands.

An operating room wasn't her natural habitat. She served, nevertheless, because she was needed. Without any formal nursing training, Sylvia learned some of the critical essentials of surgery, such as the sterile field, an area in which the actual surgery occurs, a space above the operating table framed by sterile drapes. She knew if she or anyone else touched anything outside this field, the entire area would be contaminated and the patient's health would then be in jeopardy. Sylvia was willing to endure the stuffy, pungent air caused by a bowel obstruction or cauterizing a broken blood vessel. She could hold the suture taut, and quickly hand me the surgical instrument I needed. She was good. In fact, she was *very* good, not just at assisting me in surgery, but in searching out patients who were waiting to be seen so I could take care of them between operations.

I needed Sylvia. I needed Ernie Steury. Every day was a new reminder that, for our patients and for us, Tenwek was the end of the line. That couldn't have been more real than for the Kipsigis woman who had been stabbed in the abdomen with a long machete knife. Ernie had operated on her before our arrival. He had stopped the bleeding and saved her life. The knife had penetrated deep into her abdomen, severing one of the main nerves to her right leg, before coming to rest against her lower spine. I now had to open her up. With Ernie and Sylvia's assistance, I was able to find the ends of the severed femoral nerve and suture them back together. This was specialty surgery at a mission hospital like Tenwek. Usually the pressures of time and the lack of a neurosurgeon would mean a patient like this would not receive such a major peripheral nerve repair.

It took five days to catch up on all the surgeries that had been waiting since before our arrival. Because of the jet lag and the stress and tiredness I carried with me from Ventura, I reached my limit. One morning I remember standing in the operating theater helping Ernie do an emergency operation on a young man with a bowel obstruction and wide-spread infection. The smell of his wound, the stench of the pus in the hot, stuffy room was starting to undo me. I began to feel queasy.

"I've got to drop out," I told Ernie. I needed something to eat. I needed to lie down. While I found some bread, drank some hot coffee, and searched for a bench to lie on, Sylvia scrubbed in to hold the instruments for Dr. Steury. Ten minutes later I came back in the room and saw Sylvia giving external cardiac massage, while Ernie tried to ventilate the patient. It was no use. I knew the young man was dead. The overwhelming infection and toxicity had been too much for him.

Sylvia looked pale. She was not a nurse. She had no experience with medicine or fatal illness. This was the kind of trauma she had never experienced. Barely saying a word, I took her by the hand and we walked down the hallway together. I needed to be with my best and only partner. We walked along silently and for some reason, my thoughts went back to our wedding day as we walked together down the church aisle after being pronounced husband and wife. I had been so proud of my new wife then as all of the guests watched. Now, in another lifetime, we walked together again, and the respect I had for her, the empathy I felt for her at that moment, welled deep inside me.

We found the small room where the sterile instrument packs were stored. When the door was closed, Sylvia burst into tears. As I held her close I thought of all the people in the world who have so much and may not care or don't know about the needs of hurting families in forgotten towns and cities who go to sleep every night with so little. For a moment, I wondered what Sylvia and I were doing here along with Ernie and Sue Steury and all the others who labored at this place and all the other Tenweks I would never visit. I wondered if what we were doing really mattered.

I thought of Bill Martin, who had so eagerly agreed to come here because he knew he could help someone else. That's the kind of person he is. He was standing next to me when an unconscious eight-year-old boy was brought into the outpatient clinic and suddenly went into cardiac arrest. For forty-five minutes we ventilated him and gave external cardiac massage. As the minutes lengthened, I knew we were going to lose. I took Bill by the arm. "Come on, let's give it up," I told him.

"No," he said. But death had already won. Bill stood back. He could see it. He turned around, and rushed down the hall. And then he wept. We had no idea what disease or problem had caused the boy's death. We didn't even know his name. I put my arm around Bill's shoulder, and I could tell he wanted to talk. "It's no easier here than at home to see a child die in spite of doing all we can to save him."

As I held Sylvia, I felt the tears that belonged to Tenwek. I had seen so much pass before me, the undeserving sicknesses and unlikely recoveries. For every young, helpless man I had watched die of infection, I had seen a fragile twelve-year-old smile again. When I wanted to forget all the burned children who needed skin grafts, I could remember the one-legged cancer victim who had walked through the fire of affliction, and who had shown me how to accomplish so much even with so little. And all of a sudden I realized that all of it mattered.

I heard a knock on the supply room door. I opened it and saw Marilyn Van Kuiken, the missionary midwife nurse at Tenwek. "You'd better come right away. There's a lady who is in hard labor. During a forceful contraction, she screamed with sudden, unbearable pain." Sylvia and I walked quickly out of the room and down the hall as Marilyn continued describing the problem.

"I think she has a ruptured uterus. The baby's in distress and the mother's blood pressure is falling. Now she seems in shock and I can't hear the baby's heartbeat any longer."

In moments I was next to the mother. I pulled the sheet down and felt her abdomen. There were two large protuberances. I wondered if it might be twins. After placing the girl on the operating table, I did a quick spinal anesthetic, scrubbed my hands and opened her abdomen. As the scalpel blade slid through the peritoneal lining, I could see hair! I opened the abdominal cavity wider and I saw the head of the baby lying free among the intestines. It was just as Marilyn had suspected. The uterus had split wide open during a hard labor contraction. I had to get the baby out. Clamping the umbilical cord, I removed this tiny, new breathing life and laid it in Marilyn's waiting hands. The uterus was bleeding briskly now from the long tear. I took a running suture of catgut and closed the rent. The bleeding stopped. The baby boy, now breathing with the help of oxygen, was going to live. So was the mother. Did it matter what we were doing on this quiet, forgotten slope in eastern Kenya? To a mother and her newborn child it did.

I was seeing the extraordinary become commonplace. There was the seventeen-year-old boy who had been attacked by a hippo. He was walking down by the river at night when he heard a noise and shined his flashlight into the dark. There, he saw a hippo standing a few yards away. The animal charged. The young man, turning to run, fell. In a moment of frozen panic the hippo bit down on the boy's arm and leg, all in one bite.

Fortunately the hippo walked away, but the deep puncture wounds in his arm, hip, and thigh left the boy with some paralysis in his left arm. Miraculously the wounds all healed well.

There was a Kipsigis schoolteacher, Nora Salat, who had severe disabling back and leg pain due to a pinched sciatic nerve. I operated on her spine and removed the ruptured disc to relieve her pain. Within a few days, she walked out of Tenwek, and hasn't had further problems since.

And there was the little girl who was pulled from the river as she was about to drown. She was unconscious when they brought her to Tenwek on the first day the intensive care unit was open. Ordinarily, Nellie Mac, the doctor who treated her, would not have been there. But that day she was and the girl made a complete recovery.

Years after I held the suture in my hands and removed my sweaty fingers from the surgical gloves, the faces of these people are as crisp and vivid as the picture of Tenwek that hangs on the wall at home. So is the certainty of what I experienced in the operating room: I was not alone. In the preparation and care of every patient, in the prayers that were said before each surgery, in the finely-tuned moments when a tumor was removed, tissue joined, and wounds closed, God was present. It was a reality, a calm too impossible to explain and too apparent to ignore. None of us who saw these patients surpass our best human hopes for recovery could take credit.

The days counted down to another departure. On one of my final evenings in the operating theater I realized how soon I would be leaving Tenwek. Standing in this place soon would be a longer-term surgeon, someone I didn't even know. I hoped he or she would be someone who would walk into this room, stand over this operating table, and touch hurting human lives as profoundly as the Kipsigis had touched mine.

Would I ever come back here again to operate? Was this the best way the Lord could use Sylvia and me to serve others?

As we prepared to leave Kenya, it became more and more clear to me that perhaps we could be the human instruments to bring medical equipment, supplies, hospital personnel, and funding to this place. Perhaps that had been our hope, but we hadn't actually realized it at the time.

When we arrived at Tenwek the first time, I had been shocked to find very little Pontocaine on hand. Now there were several dozen vials on the shelves of the supply room. They were there because I had called someone I knew who could possibly make this critical drug available. Dr. Clark Wescoe was the chairman of Sterling Drug, one of the largest drug manufacturers in the United States. Dr. Wescoe was the Dean who wouldn't consider my application for medical school until I had completed my senior year of college. Inspired by his firm, wise counsel, I took his advice and spent my senior year studying humanities in order to try to become a whole person and not just a physician. That decision led me eventually to the University of Kansas Medical School. The excellent training I received from the professors I studied under and admired I owed in part to Clark Wescoe. Twenty years later as I searched for his phone number, I knew exactly what I wanted to say to him.

My mind went back to the spring of 1956. I was standing at the lectern as emcee of the annual Nobel P. Sherwood lectureship that our medical fraternity sponsored each year. Before an audience of several hundred, I introduced the speaker, Dr. Herbert Werner, a virologist who had done pioneering work on the polio vaccine. He sat on my left. When it was time to introduce Dr. Wescoe, I looked out at the crowd and said, "I want to introduce someone you should know very well." Then I turned and looked at the man I admired so much. My mind went blank and I froze, unable to think of his name!

Wescoe seized the moment. In one continuous movement, he rose to the microphone, shook my hand, and said, "Wescoe! My name is Clark Wescoe. The dean of *this* medical school. The dean of *your* medical school. In fact this is *my* medical school." The crowd ate it up. As the laughter quieted, Dr. Wescoe turned to me. My face was still flushed, but I was, at least, breathing. He said, "Mr. Cheatham, you may have forgotten my name, but I can guarantee you that, even if I decide to let you graduate from my medical school, I'll never forget *your* name." The audience howled louder than before.

After I dialed the number, I looked at a letter I had received from him several years earlier. It said, "Dear Mel, I was in Los Angeles on business last week and heard you were practicing neurosurgery in Ventura. I'm writing to let you know I still haven't forgotten your name. Signed, Dr. Clark Wescoe, Chairman of the Board, Sterling Drug, Incorporated, New York City."

He wasn't in his office that day, but he called me later that afternoon. I told him of the urgent, ongoing medical needs of Tenwek Hospital.

"If you will contact our headquarters in New York," he said, "we'll see what we can do to help."

Sylvia and I visited Winthrop Pharmaceutical, a division of Sterling Drug. We told Kenneth Russell about Tenwek and described the critical need for Pontocaine for use in administering spinal anesthesia. He assured us that the need would be taken care of. What we didn't expect was that Sterling Drug would also donate 1.9 million capsules of the pain-killer Panadol, for use at Tenwek and other mission hospitals. Along with many others, we are very grateful for this. This medication was still being used as Sylvia and I returned home that September. Clark Wescoe had not forgotten my name, and I would certainly never forget his.

The tremendous generosity of Dr. Wescoe showed me that just one person could radically improve the quality of many peoples' lives. And by rushing the right resources to meet a critical need, untold families could benefit. Franklin Graham had understood this. His invitation to Sylvia and me to serve at Tenwek rested on the conviction that God could use individuals who were willing to serve the suffering and needy. When I was back home in Ventura, another comment of Franklin's caught my attention: "The number one killer in the world is polluted water."

I closed my eyes and thought about the muddy river near Tenwek. By boiling the water before drinking, patients and missionary staff had avoided disease, most of the time. Still, the water remained quite muddy, especially after a strong rain. Without question, without clear, pure water to drink, cook with, and bathe in, Tenwek's neighbors remained at risk.

Dr. Dean Miller had never tasted Tenwek's water, but he knew there was a serious problem. As pastor of the Palm Desert Community Presbyterian Church, east of Los Angeles, where Sylvia and I sometimes worshiped, he had become acutely aware of Tenwek's needs. One evening Dr. Miller invited Sylvia and me to have dinner with him and his wife, Carol, and Chuck and Maxine Billman. As we talked that December evening, we learned that the Billmans had been very successful in business. We also discovered they had a heart for helping others.

During dinner, we told them about World Medical Mission's at Tenwek. We first tried to explain about the nearby river—that it was the only source of water and that it was unsanitary, but without other options, the people were forced to drink and bathe in it. We described the medical challenges and profound joys we had experienced at the hospital. But each time we tried to develop another point, the Billmans would stop us and go back to the subject of the river.

"Wait a minute," Chuck said. "I am not a doctor, but I don't understand this. You mean that patients go to this hospital, sick from drinking unclean water, and then you give them more unclean, unsafe water right out of the river to drink and to bathe in? What about the missionaries? How can they stay healthy enough to take care of sick patients when they are drinking the same dirty, muddy river water themselves?"

"Something has to be done about this," Maxine joined in. "I can't imagine people having to drink muddy, polluted river water that way."

"Or to bathe in it either," Chuck added. "It isn't healthy and it doesn't make sense." Why were they going on like this? If it took that much explaining, Sylvia and I had obviously failed to convey the needs of Tenwek to this unusually inquisitive couple.

Several days later Chuck and Maxine Billman called us. They had decided to pay the cost of drilling wells and installing a fresh water system at Tenwek.

We had told the story of Tenwek. We had prayed long and often. Now a pair of total strangers were investing their money in the needs of a small corner of the world, in a place they had never seen, to help a hospital we didn't even know existed less than fifteen months before. Since then the Billmans have become generous supporters of Tenwek and of World Medical Mission, and close personal friends to Sylvia and me. Our unplanned meeting was the most unpredictable, unplanned twist yet in our African sojourn.

But it confirmed our previous hunches. Sylvia and I were becoming links in a global connection of Christian believers—some we knew intimately and some we didn't know at all. It was a slowly emerging phenomenon that had little to do with us and everything to do with a purpose that was much bigger and broader than any of the participants could have imagined. This included a work crusade team of twelve people from our home church, Community Presbyterian in Ventura, and Nora Caffrey, a nursing friend from Oxnard, California, who accompanied Sylvia and me for a second time of service in less than a year.

When we returned to Tenwek that next June, we saw promises fulfilled and faith at work. A five-unit apartment building to house more missionary staff had been completed. This had been paid for in part by people from the Palm Desert Community Presbyterian Church. Drilling was underway for the fresh water system, funded by the Billmans. The work crusade was already on site and completing needed construction projects of all kinds. On the team was another anesthesiologist, Dr. Bob Byers, from Yuba City, California.

As I looked around at the new facilities and the people who were building a new place at Tenwek, I couldn't help thinking about Stanley Cheborge. I was looking at his dream being fulfilled. This was the model of evangelism and Christian compassion he desired for a hospital and orphanage near the remote village of Londiani. In the few months since he had died, his dream still lay fallow on fifty now-abandoned acres he had spent his final months to secure.

My picture of Stanley became jarred suddenly by a call from the operating theater: "Dr. Cheatham, can you come, please. We have a man who is badly injured."

It was Sunday afternoon, and I had hoped to rest and begin to write down some things about Stanley's life. Suddenly this all became secondary. I walked quickly over to the operating theater. There, a man of about thirty was lying on the table. Blood was streaming from a long gash just above his right eyebrow. I could see brain oozing out like toothpaste from a tube. Blood was filling his right eye, although when I wiped it away, I could see the eye was still intact. He was alive, but barely. Despite such a terrible injury, he was even awake.

"He fell from the top of his grass-covered hut," said the friends who had brought him in. "He landed on his face and hit the blade of a hoe lying on the ground."

It was clear that the sharp, muddy blade had fractured his skull and penetrated deep into his brain. Such a "barnyard injury" would be a bad thing to deal with anywhere. Being at Tenwek made the problem seem even worse. Fortunately, Dr. Bob Byers was there. He could administer a general anesthetic so the man would be asleep during the operation. This would make the surgery easier and safer.

But as we began to contemplate the operation, we realized Bob wasn't around; he had gone to one of the nearby villages for church and had decided to walk the several miles back to Tenwek. We had to move quickly. The bleeding was so brisk and the risk of infection so great that surgery had to be done quickly.

Nora Caffrey began to get the neurosurgical instruments ready. A visiting medical student from Harvard University started an intravenous line. We were minutes away from starting, and still no Dr. Byers. I started to feel uneasy about going ahead with the operation. But why? There was almost never an anesthesiologist at Tenwek Hospital and surgical operations had to be done every day. The only thing left to do was go ahead using local anesthesia and sedation. And pray.

A Sunday evening prayer meeting had just begun in the nearby hospital chapel. While surgery was only moments away, someone told Sylvia, Nora, and me that about forty missionaries and nationals were praying for this young man.

"He is coming!" a voice called. "Dr. Byers is coming down the road toward the hospital." It was the best news I had heard all day. Someone in the doorway of the operating theater had seen him. Bob quickly put on a surgical cap and mask and administered the anesthesia that put the young, injured patient to sleep. Philip, a nurse, began to scrub the man's face and scalp.

One prayer had been answered. As I looked over the fragile situation in front of us, I knew one prayer would not be enough.

With Sylvia's help I opened the gaping scalp wound wider, removing damaged brain and pieces of bone as I worked. We went down about two inches into the brain. First, I cleaned the cavity. Then, I stopped the bleeding. Using some of the pericranium, the lining of the bone, I repaired the brain's covering. We wired together pieces of bone from the part of the skull that made up the roof of the eye socket. With a piece of fat taken from the patient's left thigh, I packed the frontal sinus between the eyes so cerebrospinal fluid from around the brain wouldn't leak out the nose later. After I trimmed up the ragged edges of scalp around the laceration, and completed the necessary plastic surgery that would enhance the man's appearance, I began to think: The brain will surely get infected. The patient will probably do poorly.

The next day, when I walked into the men's ward, I saw the young man sitting up in bed. Surprisingly, he denied even having a headache. By the second day, he was sitting outside enjoying the fresh air and sunshine. On the seventh day after his surgery, the man whose future had looked so tragic, walked out of Tenwek Hospital, without paralysis and without complaint. He was smiling, and, cosmetically, his wound looked pleasing. Because of prayer, because the Lord had looked after him, this man was a walking miracle.

I had seen God work, again. I had come back to a place of simple faith. I had learned once more the meaning of Tenwek, *"WE TREAT—JESUS HEALS."*

In the twilight of my career, I would learn this mystery once again.

TEN

I could imagine the tumor.

It would be lodged against the left side of Lilly Tesot's spinal canal, severely displacing the delicate spinal cord toward the right. The myelogram I had performed earlier revealed it was located in the mid-portion of the spine, just below the level of the shoulder blades. I judged it was probably only one inch long and a half inch in diameter. But in this definite location, very careful surgery was required if I was to remove it without further damage to the spinal cord. Thirty minutes after the first incision I would get my first glimpse of the tumor, and only then would I have a good idea about whether or not it was malignant.

Lilly Tesot sat in the wheelchair that had taken her into the operating theater. She seemed unusually calm for a woman who was about to have her spine operated on. We were moments away from surgery when Joseph Mutai, a surgical technician, said, "Let us pray." I had prayed before every surgery at Tenwek. And I knew the safety and success of Lilly's operation rested in my hands only because we were now placing her ultimate care in the hands of the Great Physician. As Joseph finished, Lilly looked up with beaming eyes and a wide smile.

It was a look that said she totally trusted in the Lord for the ordeal which would follow.

Bill Martin and the national surgical technicians moved Lilly to the operating table. He placed the anesthesia mask over her face and injected several medications into her intravenous line. Soon she was asleep. A long anesthesia tube, inserted deeply into her throat, would be her life line during the operation. For the next three hours, the only movement of her tall, slender body would be the quiet rise and fall of her rib cage.

After the operation would come the question. As the anesthesia lost its grip, Lilly would regain consciousness, and her dark world would be turned into the hazy images of the women's ward. Then she would want to know about the tumor that had left her paralyzed from the waist down: "Will I be able to walk again?"

I didn't know it at the time, but on this last day of surgery, before Sylvia and I left Tenwek in July, 1992, Lilly Tesot lay at the center of my Tenwek experience, and at the conclusion of a story that I knew needed to be told. It is a story that affects her, though she will never understand how. It is a story that involves Stanley Cheborge, though he will never appreciate why. It is a story that belongs to the people I believe will one day come and work in this place, though I will probably never know who they are. In my final few hours at Tenwek I saw my story, my life coming full circle, and I began to know Mel Cheatham in a way I never could before. It had happened in the months and minutes leading up to Lilly's surgery.

Fifteen minutes. That's all the time Sylvia and I had been at Tenwek when Cindy Tolan, the designated hostess for short-term physicians and families, arrived with our keys to the hospital and guest quarters. We had returned to Tenwek for the eighth time. After a long plane ride, I was ready to sit. That's when Cindy looked at me and said, "Mel, I don't know if you feel up to it after your long journey, but Carlos Somoza is the only surgeon here today, and he said to tell you he's swamped with cases. Do you think you could give him some help?"

Why was I not surprised? This was still the major hospital for more than a third of a million people, a place that operated morning, noon and night in a land where the needs never slept. Once we drove up to Tenwek's entrance, I knew my time belonged to someone else. This was the unchanging reality of a hospital where scores of people with serious health problems needed medical care yesterday.

I walked briskly up the hill to the operating theater and found Carlos engrossed in a thyrodidectomy, which he was doing under local anesthesia, since there wasn't anything else available. "Hello, Carlos," I said, as I tied the surgical mask around my face.

"My friend," he responded, "it is good to see you here at Tenwek. There is a young boy in the next operating theater who has a very bad leg fracture. Would you do that case?"

"Yes," I said. I walked into the next room and took a look at the boy's X-rays. Then I examined his painful, swollen knee. I could see he had a very bad fracture of his distal thigh bone, and there were displaced bone fragments. Without surgery, this boy might well end up with one leg shorter than the other. It was necessary to properly reduce the fractured bones and then maintain them in proper position until they could heal.

Bill Martin had now arrived to join me and administered a spinal anesthetic. After prepping and sterily draping the leg, I drilled a Steiman pin through the upper tibial bone, below the knee, leaving about two inches of the steel pin protruding out each side of the leg. Carlos came in the operating theater in time to hold traction on the pin while I applied pressure to reduce and realign the fractured bones. The X-ray confirmed an excellent alignment, so I drilled another steel pin through the femoral bone above the fracture. Finally, Carlos and I applied a plaster cast to the leg. This would hold the two metal pins apart to help reduce the fracture.

I could afford to relax a little. The surgical part of the procedure was now behind us. I knew I was tired. Twelve hours of night flying had left me weary with jet lag. Still, I kept going. The plaster just needed some final smoothing with water. Then I felt it. A sharp stab in my left hand!

"Owwwww!" I shouted, as my arm recoiled.

It was the tip of one of the steel pins sticking out—the end which had passed through the patient's leg!

"Oh, no!" Carlos said. "This can be very bad." Concern spread across his face. "We must hope this boy does not have AIDS. I do not think so, but it is possible. We must do a test."

Five years before, there were no cases of AIDS at Tenwek, at least that we were aware of. Now, the world had changed. Now AIDS was a fact of life. It was no longer something "out there." AIDS was exactly what I had heard it to be—a growing, worldwide epidemic with no known cure, expected to affect as many as 100 million people by the year 2000. Every six months, the number of identified AIDS cases was doubling. At this moment the statistics seemed too real.

A cold chill went through my body as I quickly removed the torn surgical glove, and poured alcohol on the wound. Next, I rubbed iodine into the cut realizing this probably would accomplish nothing except to make my hand sore. There wasn't anything to do but go on with the surgery before us. I kept saying to myself, "This boy is only thirteen years old. It's very unlikely he has AIDS." But I didn't know for sure. Suddenly, I wasn't just concerned for my own safety, I worried about other health care workers around the world who might literally be touched by this terrible disease.

Thirty minutes went by. The surgery continued. An hour went by. Then, the word came back back on the test results of the boy's blood specimen: "Negative." "Thank you, Lord," I prayed to myself. "Thank you that this little boy does not have AIDS."

The relief I felt was almost total. The little corner of the world where I now stood was no longer immune from this and other life-threatening diseases. Cancer had taken my patient and friend, Stanley Cheborge, and now it was possibly threatening Lilly Tesot. How ironic that this terrible disease had even touched the physician who began the hospital where Lilly's surgery was now moments away. Ernie Steury had worked at Tenwek for over twenty-five years with few serious health problems. In 1985, while in Indiana on furlough, doctors discovered a tumor in his colon. After surgery, doctors felt they had removed it all. But after two days, Ernie started feeling pain in his abdomen. More surgeries followed, first for an obstructed bowel, then for pelvic infection. The cancer would not leave gently. This man who had helped bring healing to hundreds, now found himself the patient.

Throughout his trips back to the U.S., through difficult surgeries that lasted up to five hours, Ernie was prayed for by thousands of people around the world. One of these was Bob Hendricks, whose daughter, Debbie, served as a missionary with World Gospel Mission. Bob had thought about calling Ernie and praying for him over the phone. But he wouldn't rest until he and Debbie drove all night from Marion, Indiana to Charlotte Memorial Hospital, where Ernie lay. At his bedside they annointed their friend with oil and prayed for his healing.

A few days later, Ernie Steury left the hospital. Several days later he found himself sitting at the dinner table, overwhelmed by the smell of chicken and rice his wife, Sue, had prepared. For the first time in nearly six weeks, Ernie brought food to his lips, a spoonful of chicken broth. By that evening, since no fluid had drained from a stomach tube, Ernie realized the obvious. The obstruction that had caused him so much pain had miraculously been relieved. When he called the surgeon the next morning and told him what had happened, the surgeon admitted, "God had to do it, because I couldn't."

Ernie's illness reminded me that friends grow old, bodies weaken, and careers give way to other, younger colleagues. As I looked around the operating theater, moments away from Lilly's surgery, I saw the changing world of Tenwek. Ernie Steury, Bill Martin and I represented an older generation of physicians. In Carlos Somoza, Dan Tolan, and many of the new doctors at Tenwek, lay the promise of the future. They and their spouses would be the next generation of medical missionaries to carry on the work which had started as an experiment in faith more than thirty years ago.

It began when a young doctor named Ernie Steury and his wife, Sue, came to this area in 1959. The experiment called Tenwek Hospital which Ernie Steury founded, had grown. It had become a watershed of healing and hope for thousands of patients thanks to a steady stream of medical personnel who arrived as strangers and left Tenwek linked to one another in a common bond of medicine and faith. They included Bob Wesche, Marty Graber, Carlos Somoza, Shaw Yount and Dick Morse. On paper they were simply names from different parts of the U.S. and the world I would rarely, if ever, visit. But at Tenwek Hospital, our lives had touched. In a place that has never seen rush hour freeways and exhausted Daytimers, I discovered a new kind of urgency that left me pleasantly exhilarated. It cut across state boundaries, college alma maters and our individual ways of practicing medicine. Remarkably, it surfaced in some of the worst possible moments, this invisible thread that Tenwek Hospital had woven into each of our lives.

I saw this thread in Carlos Somoza one morning on our last trip to Tenwek. A young man had been brought in late at night with multiple panga knife wounds to his face, neck, and right arm. The most dangerous one was the long gash across the top of his head. It was from the final blow meant to kill him. The knife had fractured his skull and driven a large piece of the bone down against the brain. Long after the sun had gone down, Carlos spent several hours meticulously suturing these many lacerations, trying to save the man's life. By morning, it was clear the cuts would heal. He would live.

I saw this invisible thread in Bob Wesche as he walked up the hill to the hospital from his quarters. He had made this trek at all hours of the day and night. Because Bob suffered from a severely degenerated hip socket, I knew how painful this was for him. Yet, I never heard him complain. He always had a smile and a kind, compassionate word for everyone he met.

Measured by my American culture's expectation of building financial security and equating self-worth with status, my Tenwek colleagues from Ernie Steury on down would be labeled failures. Instead of building a lucrative medical practice in the U.S., Ernie and Sue had decided to go to an area of the world that had never been served by an American doctor. Rather than putting in their time of one or two years, they remained at Tenwek for more than three decades. Instead of starting a practice in his native Argentina, Carlos Somoza decided he would learn three different languages—English, Swahili and Kipsigis—just to be able to treat the sick in mission hospitals.

What did the Steurys and the Somozas think they were doing? What could be more preposterous than saying No to making more money in the U.S. for the chance to fly to the other side of the world to treat poor, nameless strangers, most of whom they would never see again? I think the reason behind their decision is this: At some point in life, each of these persons heard about a little-known Jewish man who arrived at the synagogue one day, and before His city's most esteemed religious leaders unrolled a scroll and boldly declared:

"The Spirit of the Lord is upon me, because He has anointed Me to preach the gospel to the poor. He has sent me to proclaim liberty to the captives and recovery of sight to the blind, to set at liberty those who are oppressed, to proclaim the acceptable year of the Lord's favor." (Luke 4:18–19).

Not only did He believe these words, He lived them. Once claiming to be God, once declaring to be on the side of the poor and oppressed, once offering eternal life to all who believed He was the Christ, once having been crucified on a cross and then laid to rest in a cave, Jesus Christ did the most preposterous thing of all: He came back to life. Then, for almost six weeks, He met with His followers, and before rising into the clouds, He commanded them to keep His movement alive by spreading His message of forgiveness and the promise of eternal life to every corner of the earth.

On the late nights when I looked through the window and saw Bob Wesche working into the dawn trying to save a patient's life, I realized what made my decision to come here so preposterous: I had come to Tenwek because I believed in Jesus Christ. I was here because, in my forties, I stopped playing church and began wondering, "Is there more to following God than repeating Bible verses and knowing all the hymns by heart? Is there something more to being a Christian than telling other people what you believe, then hoping your life matches up with your words?" The conclusion I came to was that true Christianity is not just saying "Yes, I believe in Jesus," then living a good, moral life. True Christianity is making the choice to say, "Yes, I will follow you, Jesus, wherever you call me, because my life belongs to you." For me, this has been the decision of a lifetime.

In the loss of my earliest childhood friend I learned that people die, and that someday so would I.

In the uncommon love of my pastor, Ed Wright, I figured that being a Christian had something to do with putting love into action, because I saw it lived out before my eyes.

In the compassion of my professor and friend, Dr. William Williamson, I discovered a Christian doctor could spread this love of Jesus with the world's poor, and make a difference.

And in the invitation of Franklin Graham to combine my faith and medical practice to serve this Jesus, I realized I had no choice but to say Yes, and go wherever He called me and my family. By taking this step, I found the Christian life to be less of an obligation and more of an adventure than I ever imagined.

Now, on the last day of surgery, I looked around the operating room at my colleagues and realized I was part of something that was bigger than myself. At the operating table where Lilly Tesot lay, I was standing where Ernie Steury and Bob Wesche and others had stood before me. The common thread that connected all of us was more than a shared commitment to medicine; it was a passionate, growing desire to walk with Jesus Christ. There was simply no other way to explain the actions of these individuals. Why, for instance, would Ernie Steury drag himself out of bed at 2:00 a.m., after working non-stop for seventy-two hours, just to see one more patient? I'm sure he didn't do this because it felt good. Neither he nor any one of us stayed at Tenwek because it was comfortable or convenient. The water in the bathroom shower was cold. There was no neighborhood grocery store down the street where you would find your favorite snack. At Tenwek, as at other mission hospitals, days were long and naps almost extinct.

People like Ernie and Bob were not alone in their conviction to stay at Tenwek regardless of personal sacrifice. No one knew this better than Marty Graber, the physician who welcomed me to Tenwek. For over ten years, Marty worked in the hospital's infectious disease wards. Every day, he was exposed to TB patients. Though no longer common in the U.S., tuberculosis has been rampant in Kenya, with over half the country's population carrying TB germs.

In July 1991, after returning to the U.S., Marty began to feel discomfort in his back. A hot shower would reduce the pain, yet over the following weeks his discomfort grew, and he became bedridden. In September, Marty lost the function of his legs. He had tuberculosis of the spine, the result of serving 500 TB patients annually at Tenwek. To relieve the pain, he endured two surgeries, one to draw the infection from his spine, the other to implant metal rods in his thoracic vertebrae. Without these operations, he would have remained paralyzed from the waist down.

By May of 1992, Marty was able to walk without a brace. Instead of feeling bitter, he was already looking ahead with great expectancy. "My desire is to go back to Tenwek and help AIDS patients as much as possible. They have a need like everyone else. They know at some point they're going to die, and because of this, they are generally much more open than others to receive Christ. My goal is to make sure every patient who's come in contact with AIDS can receive Christ as Savior; that's where the real healing takes place."

Ann Graber has shared her husband's journey and continues to walk with him. "Even though Marty would be restricted, it would be hard to say No to the possibility of returning," she says. "It's always been easier going to a place like Tenwek, where there's so little, materially, than coming back to the U.S., where there's so much. I've come home to Indiana and realized I can do without a car and a television. At Tenwek, the real necessities of life are helping people. The challenge for me has been not to get so caught up in all the pressing health needs of patients that I neglect to share with them the love of Christ."

As a nurse, a wife, and a mother, Ann Graber has followed her heart to Tenwek. She and Marty have made the journey to serve—and may well make it again. It has cost them their health and time with their two children they will never get back. Their sacrifices have been real. So has the joy of giving their lives to others who do without. Perhaps that's why they'll likely return to Tenwek, and why I admire them so much.

When I picture Marty and Ann, I see others like Bob and Dora Wesche, Bill Martin, Carlos Somoza, Nora Caffrey, Judy Streamer and Nellie Mac, people who all came to Tenwek because each had heard Jesus speaking to them when He said, "You shall love the Lord your God with all your heart, and with all your soul and with all your mind. . . . This is the first and greatest commandment. And the second is like it: You shall love your neighbor as yourself" (Matt. 22:38-39). Each of these friends has taught me how God uses ordinary people. Pat Chaney is one such person. Sylvia and I met her on a crowded street in Seoul, South Korea, on our first overseas trip with World Medical Mission. What made it so unusual is that Pat lives in Ventura and attended Community Presbyterian Church, where we worship. We had to travel half way across the world to meet a neighbor! The only thing more obvious than Pat's infectious laugh is her unselfish heart. After we told her about our work at Tenwek, and shared how she could help patients, she paid her way and accompanied us on two of our return trips. As long as she can arrange her schedule as a school teacher, she remains ready to return to Tenwek.

The people of Tenwek Hospital, from the founders at World Gospel Mission onward, weren't in it for themselves. Rather, they had experienced the most powerful force on the planet, the love of Jesus Christ that caused them to serve others. I could see the evidence of this conviction all around me, because of what it had built.

The current hospital building that houses male and female surgery wards, pediatrics and the operating theaters, was built in 1985 after Franklin Graham visited Tenwek, and then told a nationwide U.S. television audience what was needed to overcome the tremendously overcrowded conditions he had seen. The result was $265,000 in gifts, much of it in one dollar bills, mailed in by hundreds of concerned Christians.

The Johanna Ngetich Medical Center added beds and provided two major operating rooms and a minor operating room. Improved pediatric space, men's and women's surgical wards, and a small intensive care unit helped reduce the patient occupancy rate by 104 percent in one year.

The Edna Boroff Maternity Building is a testament to the missionary nurse who has helped deliver more than 18,000 babies during her forty years at Tenwek. This facility increased the number of maternity beds from thirty-three to eighty and doubled the size of the labor and delivery areas.

The Community Health Program, started by Dr. David Stevens and Susan Carter, R.N., brought dramatic improvement in treating basic communicable diseases and health problems. Hospital admissions for measles, which reached 600 in 1983, had dropped to just over 21 in 1988. Whooping cough cases fell from 160 to 20 in the same time. And admissions for diarrhea which peaked at 2,500 in 1985, had fallen to 500 annually, largely because people had been taught to boil their drinking water and practice better sanitation. Volunteer "health helpers" have continued teaching local residents about preventing burns and malaria, family planning, immunizations, first aid, and the importance of a clean home.

Today, families proudly display a "Healthy Home Certificate" on the walls of their huts for having changed five health behaviors. Through the Community Health Department that takes the program to outlying villages, over 10,000 people each year receive Christ, while many others have been discipled in their faith.

The Nursing School, begun by American nurses Mary Hermiz and Barbara Pinkley, trains male and female nurses and has attracted the attention of Kenya's national health care leaders. As a result, the number of nurses increased from six in 1987 to twenty-five in 1991, and the quality of care has continued to rise.

A new outpatient facility has helped meet the flood of 30,000 to 40,000 incoming patients a year. No longer are they led to small, cramped examining rooms, but to larger areas where good examination and modesty are no longer the exception but the rule. Against the backdrop of these new buildings and the activity inside them, the most life-transforming efforts seem almost invisible. From 1987 through 1992, under the leadership of Senior Chaplain David Kilel, the Christian Evangelism ministry of Tenwek brought the Gospel to nearly 150,000 people. And over 57,000 of these accepted Jesus Christ as their personal Lord and Savior.

I had good reason to believe Lilly Tesot was one of these people. Stretched out on the operating table in front of me, she must have been six feet tall. Like most Kipsigis, she barely made a sound. She could not speak or understand a word of English. Paralyzed from the lower rib cage downward, she lived with a constant throbbing pain in her mid-spine and chest. Yet you wouldn't have known it by her peaceful manner.

Before the surgery I had told her the seriousness of what we were dealing with. "I am sure you have a bad thing, a tumor, growing in your spine, causing you to lose the use of both of your legs. The only chance for improvement is with an operation to find the problem, and then try to remove it."

When the translator's words reached Lilly, she looked at me without the slightest bit of anxiety. Her voice remained soft and unshaken. "I know God will take care of me." This poor, uneducated woman was placing her complete trust in God. Materially, she had almost nothing, yet she had everything she needed. When Jesus said, "Many who are first will be last, and the last first," (Matt. 19:30) He was talking about Lilly Tesot. I thought about how tall she stood in the Lord's eyes.

The anesthesia lowered her into a calm, painless sleep. We positioned her on her abdomen with blanket rolls under her hips. Suddenly, I remembered Stanley, and I was standing at the place where I had started my journey. This was the same operation I had done on his spine six years earlier. Like Ernie Steury had experienced so many times before me, I was standing at the end of the line because Tenwek Hospital was Lilly Tesot's last best chance to get well. Back in the United States, plenty of neurosurgeons would have been eagerly waiting to operate on her. At Tenwek I stood in a line of one. If I didn't do the surgery, it wouldn't get done. Without surgery, Lilly would live the rest of her life unable to move her legs. She would have no control over her bladder.

With surgery, there was hope she might be able to walk again—if the tumor was benign, and if I could get it all. However, being at the end of the line meant there were risks. I would have to operate without any blood supply available for transfusion because of her less common blood type. If Lilly began bleeding excessively, we would be in trouble. I had none of the microsurgical instruments I normally used on such an operation back home. Without a surgical operating microscope, I would work with magnifying glasses, which had only two and one-half times the power. There was no CT or MRI scan to help identify the nature and size of the tumor. Instead, I had to rely on a limited myelogram to help diagnose her condition.

A neurosurgeon used to the most sophisticated conditions and equipment in the U.S., well aware of the risks, might have said to me, "How can you possibly go ahead with surgery when there is so much you lack?" I looked around me and thought, "How can I *not* proceed when I have so much?" I had the luxury of an anesthesiologist in Bill Martin. I had the help of an experienced assistant in my wife, Sylvia. And I had something else, a living example of faith in Lilly Tesot.

As the surgery began, Ernie Steury, Dan Tolan and Carlos Somoza each stood behind me, eager to learn. "We are certainly glad you are here to operate on this patient," Ernie said. "Without you, we wouldn't be able to do this surgery," added Carlos. His words were a confirmation of my own growing belief that I was exactly where I needed to be. As a neurosurgeon I was bringing years of experience to a highly-specialized procedure I knew would have been a real challenge for a non-neurosurgeon.

I made the incision and began the process of removing part of the spine. Exposing the spinal cord sac, I could see the cause of Lilly's paralysis. As I suspected, the tumor was compressing her spinal cord. Being a neurofibroma, it was separate from the spine, and causing paralysis. The good news was it was benign, and I knew I would be able to remove it. Whether the paralysis would resolve with time and Lilly would walk again, I wasn't so sure.

As I began to take out the tumor, I felt company. A person whose voice I knew was talking to me. "Be careful with that curette; it can be a deadly instrument!" In a distant corner of my mind I could hear Dr. Charles Brackett instructing me. He was my professor of neurosurgery back in medical school and residency training. Since that time he and his wife, Donna, had remained our special friends. Now, it was as if he were standing at my side. As with Dr. Williamson, I frequently seemed to almost hear them offering me advice, instruction, or admonition while operating. After the intense years of training I'd spent with both men, I was careful with the curette, a six-inch-long metal instrument with a small, sharp curve on the end.

I knew my mentors were looking on. I dissected out the inside of the tumor; this reduced its size enough so that its capsule could be teased away from the spinal cord. Within two hours the surgery was over. The hospital record would show that Dr. Melvin L. Cheatham had performed the surgery. But I knew I'd had assistance from Drs. Brackett and Williamson.

Within minutes after the last suture was tied, Lilly Tesot opened her eyes. She said she could feel some sensation in her legs. There was still no movement, but with time I felt this could come. Now, at least she had a chance.

"Thank God for bringing you through the operation safely," I said to her. "And pray that in time, you will regain the use of your legs."

"I will pray," she responded.

The next morning, I examined Lilly, and the sensation in her lower extremities had improved even further. She now had slight movement in both legs. By the end of the day, she had begun to move her feet and toes slightly. That night, as I said goodbye, I could tell by her smile that Lilly Tesot must have been the happiest person in Kenya. I learned her recovery, like so many others, was not based entirely on the skill of the surgeon, but on the "something else" Lilly believed in that helped make healing possible—prayer.

When I found myself asking, "Is anything we're doing here really making a difference?" I looked at Lilly, and I knew the answer was Yes.

And she was not the only one. A few days earlier, Marilyn Van Kuiken reminded me of the time months before on an earlier visit here, she rushed in with news of an expectant mother in great pain. The woman's uterus had ruptured and she was minutes away from losing the baby. By doing emergency surgery, the child and the mother both lived. Marilyn hadn't forgotten the experience. "I thought you'd like to know, Mel, the baby you delivered that morning is now a healthy, growing boy."

What we were doing at Tenwek Hospital did make a difference. Every minute mattered, because every day brought the possibility that a life could be saved, a limb mended and a person made a little more whole. I felt privileged to observe such daily miracles that happened even when the lack of medicine, or the equipment needs said "It's impossible." Daily miracles took place because those of us who labored at Tenwek knew our human hands could do only so much. If we lacked guidance, wisdom, or patience, we knew where to find it. As a result, I saw patients walk out of Tenwek, some completely well, others still on the painful path to recovery. And whether they walked alone, or with family, I knew Jesus was walking with them.

One patient did not walk out of Tenwek under his own power. Stanley Cheborge had been carried by his brothers and placed into a combi-van. Then, after being driven over twenty unkind miles that made his pain even worse, he was brought home for the final time. After the operation on Lilly and after the last surgery wrapped up and I pulled off the last pair of rubber gloves, I knew there was one more thing I had to do. I was going to retrace Stanley's journey and travel to his home. Six years after his death, we would visit his family in their hut near the Maasai border. I had made two previous trips to Stanley's home. Both still generated unpleasant memories. The first had been to see Stanley while he stretched out on the hard earth, still determined he would walk away from cancer. It was the last time I saw him.

The second visit took place three years later, in June, 1989. I had gone to the Cheborge's hut expecting to renew a friendship with Stanley's father. What began so calmly inside the father's darkened hut rapidly built into one of the most emotionally-charged and revealing experiences of my life.

Stanley Cheborge had been our friend, and we had felt called to visit his family. Ernie and Sue Steury and David Kilel joined Sylvia and me on the trip to Lelaitich. I remember sitting in the semi-darkness of the tin-roofed hut. Against the mud-walled interior, I could see Mr. Cheborge begin to move. He was an elderly man, yet muscular and powerful. First there were the arms, waving wildly. Then he began giving what sounded like a stern lecture, all in Kipsigis, of course.

He moved around the dirt floor, words flying from his mouth. They were filled with pain and grief. Ernie and Sue knew Kipsigis. I glanced at them on my left, and both had tears in their eyes. What were they hearing from this anguished man? All I could do was sit by as both a spectator and a front-row participant in a raging drama that kept me startled and perplexed.

Arap Cheborge rolled on like a violent storm. Only occasionally did he stop to breathe. His eyes were full of sorrow, and the large veins bulging from his stocky neck threatened to burst at any moment. Arap Cheborge was still grieving two years after the death of his son. Then, as quickly as he began, he turned, walked through a low doorway, and was gone.

I sat, still puzzled, yet starting to make sense of this man's sadness. Not only had he lost his favorite son, but he had said goodbye to his daughter-in-law, Annah, and her child, Grace. Both had escaped Kipsigis tradition which declared they automatically must live with the husband's family. Now Annah and Grace were living in Kericho, some seventy miles away, with no plans to ever return. On top of this, Arap Cheborge grieved because there was no male heir to carry on Stanley's name. His seed would not be passed on to perpetuate the lineage of the family and the tribe. He had lost a son, a family, and a heritage in one painful death.

Without fanfare, the father returned. Slowly he began to speak, and once again the grief began to build. His words crackled like sticks on fire until his face glowed like a red coal. He jumped to his feet again and slapped his thighs as if to underline his words with added fury. Once again, the explosion stopped. Once again, without warning, he burst through the opening and disappeared from sight.

My heart was pounding louder now. This time Sue Steury translated the message of the man I yearned to understand: "Stanley was his youngest, his favorite son. The one called upon by tradition to care for him in his old age. He cannot understand why Stanley had to die so young."

I looked into the eyes of Arap Cheborge, and saw my own father staring back. In a moment, he was gone from the room, leaving me to sit with a single thought: What if I had been Stanley? I can only imagine the pain my father would have felt. He had always been there for me. Whenever I scored a goal in basketball, somehow I could hear his voice above the crowd. My father kept cheering long after I graduated. When he died, I lost more than a parent. I lost a partner who gave to me more love than I was ever able to return.

He died when he was seventy-seven on a day that will always linger. Through my own sorrow, I found comfort in the fact that his life was long, and full, and that he lived in a new home with the same Lord he had come to know as a child. How much greater was Arap Cheborge's grief. He had lost a son, a young man with years of life ahead of him. And not just a son, but the offspring he cherished the most. In losing Stanley, he lost the security of knowing his youngest son would take care of him in his old age. Without Stanley, without any escape from his own inner darkness, the father grieved alone. For him, death was final. There was no heaven, no afterlife. Only a bitter, unfair end.

In this sad, flickering moment, the barrier of language fell away. In the dim interior of a mud-walled hut, I heard a father's heart breaking, as I loved my own father once again.

In what felt like a few minutes, Arap Cheborge stooped through the low entranceway. A new angst filled his eyes as he moved out from the shadows that lined the back of the hut. I thought the air would explode. A long steel blade flashed before my eyes. The father now had a knife! Sunlight from a small, high window caught the blade. Arap Cheborge froze. A look of tired defeat seemed to run from the corners of his sad, reddened eyes. After pausing for a long moment, he made a quarter turn, dropped his head, and left.

The room went silent, again. Sylvia leaned toward me and whispered, "What are we doing here?" I didn't know what to tell her. After several minutes, the father came back. This time he placed the long knife in the back of the room. He seemed calm now. He turned to David Kilel and began to speak passionately in Kipsigis. As he talked, I noticed Arap Cheborge looked repeatedly at Sylvia and me. The father paused, and then David Kilel turned to us and said, "He is asking, 'Are you true friends, or just the kind of friend who comes to visit when there is food to be served,'" We said to David, "Assure him that we were friends of his son, Stanley, and that we have continued to be friends of his family."

As David delivered my response in Kipsigis, a smile spread across the father's face. Arap Cheborge rose to his feet, clasped my hands between his and began shaking them vigorously. The bond of friendship now seemed secure. Then, as if by some unheard signal, the mother entered the hut, smiled and shook the hand of each guest. This was much more than a casual greeting. She cupped the hands of each guest between both of her hands, an indication of the greatest possible sincerity and respect. Other female family members appeared and poured water from a container, washing our hands for the dinner that followed. First, we were given a small bowl containing pieces of liver, kidney, and intestine from the goat Arap Cheborge had just killed. This was followed by a basket piled high with gimiet, boiled maize and more goat meat. We ate it all with our fingers.

Now, three years later, we were back at the same hut, with the same family. Arap Cheborge seemed much older now. He was warm, friendly, and very happy to see us. He even apologized for not knowing we were coming, otherwise, he explained he would have killed a goat. Mrs. Cheborge and the other members of the family crowded around where we sat on small wooden chairs. A cold breeze began to blow, and I shivered for the many small children who had little clothing on. We listened as Peter, one of Stanley's brothers, told us of Stanley's youth, his suffering and how his faith and trust in the Lord had sustained him. He told us of how hard life was now for his parents, since Stanley was not alive to assume his responsibility of caring for them in their old age. A few feet away I noticed the half-completed, tin-roofed hut the family was trying to build for Stanley's mother. The walls were no more than sticks planted in the ground. Because there was no money the walls remained unfinished.

It was growing dark. After Mrs. Cheborge and Esther Kilel left and returned with hot chai for us to drink as we visited, David Kilel stood. He asked me if I would say some words of greeting and then read a passage from the Bible. I looked around at this Kipsigis family I had known before and now was coming to know again, and it was not hard for me to find the right words.

"We are very happy to be here," I said. "We want to thank you for your hospitality. God has been good to us all, and we give Him great thanks for this." Then I opened the Bible and turned to a verse I knew would be short, and familiar, and yet would have great meaning to this family. "In the sixteenth verse of the third chapter of the Gospel of John we read: 'For God so loved the world that He gave His only begotten Son, that whoever believes in Him should not perish, but have eternal life'" (John 3:16).

There were smiles and nods of recognition and approval as David interpreted what I said. Peter and Michael, the two brothers present, along with Stanley's mother were Christians. Arap Cheborge still had not made this step, and I knew this had been a disappointment to Stanley.

"Let us stand and pray," said David. All of us stood in the chilly open air of the parched, drought-stricken countryside near the Maasai border as David, the senior chaplain at Tenwek, thanked God for the many blessings He had brought to us. As he finished praying, I saw looks of happiness on the faces of everyone. By the standards of the Western world, these people had so little. But by knowing the gift of God's love, they had so much.

David walked over to the father, and I could see them talking. After a while, David came over to me. "Dr. Cheatham, the father says that he will accept Jesus." A few feet away from me, I could see the spot where Stanley had been born, and where he had given up life. In this same place where Stanley had prayed for his father to know God, Arap Cheborge accepted Jesus Christ as his Savior and Lord. I knew how much Stanley would have wanted to stand next to his father when he declared his faith in Christ. If Arap Cheborge's words were true, then I knew both father and son would one day be standing together in a new home they could call their own. Forever.

We rode back to Tenwek that night with a chicken and a large ram, both gifts from the Cheborges. Even with so little, this family gave everything they had to make sure we did not go home empty-handed. As we were leaving, I could feel the night air biting. I looked at Arap Cheborge, wearing just a thin coat. I removed my navy blue blazer with the brass buttons and handed it to him. It was the one thing I had to give. I just hoped it would keep him warm.

There was rain on the windshield when we arrived at the guest house. I had been inside only minutes when a call came from the operating theater. It was Richard Kosgei, one of the Kenyan surgical technicians. "Dr. Cheatham," he asked, "Is it possible that you might come to the theater to talk with me?"

"Yes, I'll come." I knew that Richard had a gift for me. He had brought two beautifully made arrows from his tribe, and he wanted me to have them to take to our home. A few minutes later, I walked into the operating theater and there was Richard talking with some of the other nationals. The moment he saw me he excused himself and showed me to a room. He said he wanted to talk. He told me about the arrows and how finely made they were. "Your gift is very special, and I appreciate it very much," I told him.

Then Richard looked at me and said, "Those of us here in the operating theater have discussed something. We want to know when will you come to Tenwek, to stay here permanently and work with us?"

What would I say? Financially, it would not be a problem. Certainly we could make the move. We would have the prayers and support of our children and many friends. I had repeatedly been able to function as a general surgeon once more, with the help of other missionary surgeons, with prayers and with much help from the Lord.

"It would be wonderful for us to be able to stay here at Tenwek," I said to Richard. "Still we must leave . . ."

In many ways, I wished we could stay. Every day, a line of human need formed at the door of the hospital. The crying children and the silent wanting faces were a given. And so was a fact I had come to accept: I was a neurosurgeon, a specialist with a finely-focused skill. If I remained at Tenwek, the professional skills I had developed, based on the abilities and talents God had blessed me with, would generally go unused. I could keep operating here and ignore the path that now stretched before Sylvia and me. But now it was necessary us for to leave.

I said goodbye to Richard and walked back to our guest quarters. I remembered the first time I rode up the entranceway, looked around at the clusters of waiting patients and thought about waking up that next morning to begin work. Within a few minutes after our lunch with the Grabers, I found myself in the operating room. I had realized early on that in Kipsigis there are no words for "jet lag." At Tenwek, as I suspect at so many other medical outposts in the Third World today, there is only one question: "Doctor, when can you come?"

On our last night at Tenwek, how many countries, how many other communities, home to parasites and poverty, would be asking that same question as I slept? Too many. I did not turn away from this fact. Instead, I embraced it as part of a new calling to serve not just at Tenwek, but in many areas around the world. This would be a continuing walk with Franklin Graham as he responded to the needs of others through the work of Samaritan's Purse and World Medical Mission. Franklin had accepted this responsibility as president of Samaritan's Purse following the death of its founder, Dr. Bob Pierce, in 1978. After the formation of World Medical Mission by Dr. Lowell Furman and Dr. Richard Furman, two surgeon brothers from Boone, North Carolina, the organization had become the medical arm of Samaritan's Purse with Franklin as its president as well.

Wherever in the world there were people sick, or hungry, or hurting from the wounds of war, you could find Franklin. He traveled not only in the U.S. and Canada, but to the remote corners of the world seeking out those in need whom others had passed by.

With Dick Furman, I had stood beside Franklin in a Contra guerrilla camp in Honduras, as we walked down row after row of young men and women wounded in war. With Reverend Guy Davidson, former director of World Medical Mission, I had visited the mission hospital at Nyankunde in Zaire, where doctors were operating with fishing line because they had no surgical suture to sew up their patients. Guy and I had stood together at mission hospitals in Brazil where even the most basic medical equipment and supplies were critically needed.

The medical needs I found in a hurting world followed me back home to the U.S. At our World Medical Mission board meetings, I heard Dr. Robert Foster tell of the great health care needs in Angola, where he and his wife, Belva, had spent over forty years of their lives in missionary service. I listened to Elmer Kilburn, a liaison for Samaritan's Purse, speak in highly emotional tones about the incredible needs for assistance in India. And I learned of other parts of the globe where sickness and disease run rampant from Dr. David Stevens, who had returned from Tenwek to lead World Medical Mission as its director. He is trying to answer these great and growing needs of a hurting humankind.

I was coming home to the reality that Tenwek had been the first step in my journey to join a global effort I never planned. The movement had already reached into Croatia, Ethiopia, Hungary, Somalia and closer to home—the hurricane stricken coast of South Carolina. And in each of these pockets of human suffering, Franklin Graham and those who worked alongside him came with more than medical care and relief. They came preaching the Gospel of Jesus Christ.

Preparing to leave Tenwek for the last time I felt the world's needs growing larger with each day. Where are the people who are willing to do something about this? Where are the Christian doctors and nurses, the professionals and laypersons, who believe Jesus can use their skills, their lives, even their doubts and apprehensions, to bring healing to others? I know they are out there in downtown clinics and private practices, in retiring rural towns and in medical schools where graduates are still wondering about their chosen fields. If they are people like Shaw Yount, I know the world will be different.

Shaw was a recent graduate of the University of Texas School of Medicine in Houston when he first went to Kenya in 1986. While serving with World Medical Mission, and serving at Friends Lugulu Hospital in western Kenya, he visited hospitals in Uganda, Tanzania, Zimbabwe and Zambia. Along the way he found himself asking, "God, is this where I should be?" By the time I met him, Shaw had been at Tenwek six months. He stayed another year working in the maternity and pediatrics wards and wherever there was a need. In 1989, he went back to his home in Winston-Salem, North Carolina. But not to stay.

Rusitu, Zimbabwe, will be a different place soon because of Shaw and his wife, Sharon. They will be the only physicians in their mission station in an area that serves 100,000 people. They will work in a facility destroyed in the 1970s by that country's civil war. Shaw and Sharon have a vision. They want to expand a small clinic of fifteen beds into a small hospital three times the size. Like Tenwek, the people who come to the Rusitu Mission Station will learn they are loved by a God who longs to make them whole in all ways—spiritually, emotionally, and physically. Patients are met by students from an adjoining

Bible school who share the love of Jesus Christ. I am waiting for the day when Shaw and Sharon Yount welcome a visiting medical school student, a family practitioner, a general surgeon, an anesthesiologist, or a nurse who will discover how much his or her skills are needed—and know how much they are loved by those they have come to serve.

When I thought of Shaw and other medical missionaries I had met, like Drs. Michael Johnson, Daniel Tolan, Philip Renfroe, Carlos Somoza and Hal Burchel, I saw a new generation of medical missions being born. Like Ernie Steury more than thirty years earlier, they would be the only physicians for miles around, the doctor at the end of the road for the child with pneumonia and the expectant mother struggling to deliver. I thought of all the equipment and supplies they would need in order to meet even the most basic health care needs, things like antibiotics, anesthetic medications and equipment, cardiac monitors, fiber optic instruments, even surgical gloves.

It was then I realized that if doctors and nurses are to make their own commitment to go and serve at a mission hospital, they need to have the medications and at least the basic equipment with which to work once they get there. From experience, I knew that a wealth of these items lay inside the used equipment storerooms of hospitals, the warehouses of medical supply companies, and on the back shelves of pharmaceutical production lines. In these hidden caches are the things so desperately needed to help the sick in mission hospitals and clinics throughout the developing world.

This is why Franklin Graham and the Boards of Samaritan's Purse and World Medical Mission developed the L. Nelson Bell Center in Boone, North Carolina. Through this facility, named after the medical missionary who served in China for twenty-five years, and the father of Franklin's mother, Ruth Graham, medical equipment and supplies, as well as other disaster relief items can be received, crated, and shipped to places around the world where the need is great.

One of the first projects of this new Center was to provide relief supplies to the victims of the war in Croatia. At the same time, a large shipment of supplies, including a cardiac monitor, respirator, X-ray machine and numerous other items was brought to Moscow to help establish a Christian Medical Diagnostic Center. Standing with Franklin Graham and Guy Davidson in Moscow, in July, 1991, and presenting this equipment to the Russian people was one of the high points of my life.

The worlds of Russia and Rusitu reached my world of Tenwek on that last night. Six years ago I had traveled to Africa on a safari. I went to see wild animals. I came away remembering the faces of hungry, weakened Maasai children. Their faces, the flies on their bare, dusty skin, never left me. They were my first glimpse of the part of the Third World that goes to bed sick each night. Because of them, because of Tenwek, because the needs of people and the calling that had been too great to ignore, the rest of my life would never be the same.

Whenever I thought of this, I gave thanks that I had been able to help my fellow physicians on two continents—colleagues I would never know in Moscow, Russia, as well as a pioneering couple bound for Zimbabwe who were lifelong friends. Suddenly I was humbled. What had my life come to? The things I valued most I realized I had achieved: husband, father, doctor, surgeon, neurosurgeon.

I had learned very well to acquire the things I wanted. Then, when I thought I had everything to feel fulfilled, I found there were other people in the world not so much interested in acquiring. These were the givers, people who traded in their ambitions to be part of a cause, a mission, a dream that was bigger than themselves. These were people like Franklin Graham, Ernie Steury, Marty Graber, Bob Wesche and David Stevens. Good, gifted, selfless individuals who, along with their wives and families, had each given up so much of what most people consider important—security, comfort, and status—to be servants of Jesus. I continue to marvel at their commitment to serve others and not themselves. I continue to be struck by the fact that in these friends I have caught a very small glimpse of what Jesus is like. These glances of godliness only make me see how far I still have to go in learning to give myself away.

On our last morning at Tenwek, I walked down the main entrance one last time. I looked at the buildings and imagined the people inside them. My mind's eye wandered down the hallway to a familiar wooden door, and I could see myself again sitting next to a young Kipsigis man. He was lying on his side. Even though his eyes seemed tired, a look of contentment filled his face.

"Mel, we're ready to leave." Sylvia's voice reached me as I stood next to the red Land Rover that would take us to the airstrip at Bomet. I turned to look back at the hospital. In the room, I could hear Stanley's voice.

"Dr. Cheatham, I believe with all my heart the Lord will heal me. There is so much He has for me to do."

"What kinds of things, Stanley?" I asked him.

"I want to bring the Gospel to my people. I want them to hear the story of Jesus and know the great love He has for them. I want to care for those who have no one in this world—the widow, the stranger, the orphan. Someday I would like to build a home for these forgotten ones whom Jesus cares for. These are the kinds of things I want to do."

I could see myself leaning a little closer toward him, wanting to ask the question I had thought much about.

"Stanley, I think the story of your life should be told to others. Could I have your permission to tell the story to others someday?"

He looked at me, somewhat surprised. "Yes, Dr. Cheatham, if you feel someone would be interested. I would like that."

I saw myself sitting by his bed for another few moments. And then I got up and left his room for one of the last times.

The smell of exhaust fumes pulled me back to the present moment, as I realized the Land Rover would be leaving. I climbed into the vehicle and shut the door. With Cindy Tolan driving, we rolled slowly out the main entrance, and Tenwek Hospital became a shaky blur in the rear-view mirror. Down the road a single-engine plane was waiting. Less than an hour later, while the sun was still rising, we crawled inside its metal skin. Then we raced the length of the thin asphalt strip, and climbed into the clouds.

Outside my window I could see Africa, still bigger, more wandering and alive than I had seen before. As we neared the beginning of the vast Maasai Mara grasslands, I knew that Stanley's hut must be somewhere below us. I asked the pilot to dip the wings as a salute to the memory of the one-legged Kipsigis warrior I admired and respected.

Above the roar of the aircraft's engine, the pilot shouted, "Do you think your friend was down there and saw us?"

"He doesn't live there anymore," I replied. Then I looked out on the vast blue sky and soaring white clouds so far beyond earth. And I knew where my friend was.

Thank you, Stanley Cheborge. Thank you for your example. You have taught me a great deal. I will share your story in the same way you shared your life with me. Full of joy and hope.

EPILOGUE

Where We Have Walked

If I could relive one conversation with Stanley in the five short months of a friendship that changed my life forever, I know the exact spot where I would rewind the tape.

It was a warm July afternoon, and I was seated on the grass next to Stanley outside his hut. This vibrant twenty-six-year-old man exuded joy. His smile, his outlook on life, belied the fact that terminal cancer had invaded his failing body.

"Dr. Cheatham, there is so much we will never be able to tell each other, because the days aren't long enough, or long in number. But I need to share with you, again, my dream. It is a dream I have carried in my heart for as long as I can remember."

I found myself leaning forward, not quite sure of what he would say next.

"My one hope is that one day I will be able to start an orphanage and a school where children with no home and no education can grow to know the Lord. And if the Lord wills, perhaps there would be a hospital too."

Less than three months later, Stanley died on the dirt floor of his parents' mud hut. By then, however, he had shared his dream with family and friends. When I returned to Tenwek that following summer, I met some of the children Stanley talked about. They were malnourished. Many would never sit inside a classroom, learn simple addition, or write their own tribal dialect. Most would not live beyond fifty years of age. Without teachers, doctors, and other caregivers, these children would only prolong their parents' cycle of poverty and sickness.

The cycle would continue, in part, because few people in Stanley's tribe dared to dream. After all, they lacked the money and leadership to build an orphanage, or schools, much less fill them with supplies and staff them with people whom they could pay. I tried to put myself in their place. If all I knew was a mud hut, hardened earth to till, and a few animals to raise—if this is all my parents, and my parents' parents, and *their* parents had ever known—I too would never have a reason to hope for anything different. I too would come to accept hunger and disease.

Stanley dared to dream outside of these boundaries. He brought his dreams to God. In prayer, Stanley dared to agree with God, who promised to love and care for people in their most basic, daily needs.

Somehow, in a way only God could have orchestrated, Stanley's dream caught up with a missionary named Hillary Crehan. She had come to Kenya in 1983 to work with a Christian publishing group. When Sylvia and I met her in Nairobi two years later, we learned about her life and what had brought her to Kenya.

Hillary saw the tremendous need of the country's children, and founded a school north of Nairobi in the Ngong Hills. Several years later she felt called to the area called Londiani, some seventy-five miles northwest of Tenwek. Here, unaware of Stanley's dream of helping children, she began to develop a school where kids would receive an education they would otherwise be denied. Geographically, it was not a paradise. Londiani had been a stopping point on Kenya's railroad line running westward to Uganda and Zaire. Over the years, drought and ongoing tribal conflicts led to Londiani's decay. Hillary learned that in Londiani, "living on the other side of the railroad tracks," was not just an expression of speech but a sad state of existence. Lush tea plantations blanketed the region to the south, while the Londiani highlands on the opposite side were rocky and barren.

In this parched plateau, with no other agenda than to love children, Stanley's dream began to come alive, because of how God was using Hillary to carry out his plan. It took some time. The first thing she did was to build a house. Eventually there was a two-room school, followed by two more schools and additional missionary housing. The number of children, all dressed in somewhat tattered, yet brightly colored school uniforms, swelled to over 400.

Other projects followed. Franklin Graham led Samaritan's Purse to build a medical dispensary where a nurse could give shots and offer basic medical care. Today, a health center offering patient care has been constructed using rocks, lumber, and sheet metal.

Hillary was a doer and a builder. She refused to accept the words, "can't be done," when the need for food, and schooling, and Bibles was obvious. Like Stanley, she believed God has a way to meet every need. The children she reads to today (and who have learned to read to her), the children she sings and prays with are living proof that lives can and do change. The next project was to build a small satellite dispensary that provided medicines to people from the more remote areas of the surrounding countryside who would otherwise not have medical care.

One day while in Londiani I stood with Hillary as children entertained us by singing and dancing a national dance. I looked at these young faces and immediately thought of another face.

"These are the children Stanley dreamed about," I told her. "Wouldn't it be something if his dream of caring for the needs of children could happen right here?"

Suddenly I thought back to my conversation with Stanley that warm, July afternoon.

"My one hope is that one day I will be able to start an orphanage and a school where children with no home and no education can grow to know the Lord. And if the Lord wills, perhaps there would be a hospital too."

Little did Stanley know that he was writing the epilogue to his life story.

For me, the poignancy and power of Stanley's life is that he lived it without any assurances or guarantees of what tomorrow would bring. "Whatever happens to me, I know there is a God who loves me, and I will serve this God by loving others all the days of my life."

I can imagine Dr. Ernie Steury, the missionary doctor who was one of Stanley's most cherished friends, saying the same words as he, himself, battled cancer, and then returned to Tenwek Hospital to continue serving the Kenyan people.

I can hear Stanley's faith spoken in the life of Ann Graber, who, a few years after Stanley's death, lost her own life to cancer as she urged her husband, Marty, to keep serving in the mission field where the two had worked together most of their married life.

Today, I can see Stanley's faith in Marty, himself, who, after fighting and nearly being rendered paralyzed by tuberculosis of the spine, continues practicing medicine as a missionary in southern Kenya, because Marty's dream, like Stanley's, is to love others in Jesus' name.

And I see this Kipsigis tribesman's faith in a friend whose future, like Stanley's, hung in the balance . . .

I think back to the morning I re-examined Lilly Tesot, the Kenyan woman whom I had operated on for a spinal cord tumor the previous day. Although still paralyzed, she had regained the slightest movement in her toes. When I touched her feet, she experienced a slight awareness of sensation. Even so, there was no question in my mind Lilly would remain paralyzed for life.

Two years later on a return visit to Tenwek for Samaritan's Purse, I was asked to give the message at the chapel service. As I was speaking, I saw Lilly Tesot seated about halfway back in the church. I motioned to Lilly, and to my surprise she stood up!

Then, amazingly, standing tall and erect, Lilly walked down the center aisle of the chapel toward me. I had pictured her lying on the mud floor of her mud-walled hut for the rest of her life, paralyzed and unable to move her legs. Now, she was fully recovered and able to walk unaided. She stepped up on the platform and stood beside me. She was smiling brightly as she reached for my hands and clasped them tightly and lovingly in hers. There were tears in her eyes—and in mine.

It was incredible: Lilly had that same look of calmness and peace as on the morning I operated on and removed her spinal cord tumor. I had told her that she might die as a result of the surgery and that it was very unlikely the operation would help. I remember how she looked at me and said, "I have no fear, because I have the love of Jesus Christ in my heart. I know He will take care of me and if it is His will, I will live, and I will improve."

Stanley Cheborge and Lilly Tesot are bookends of a story that is still being written—in schools where children find love, in a hospital where patients receive care, and in mud-walled huts where the life of a Kipsigis tribesman shows others how to live and dream.

Years ago, I climbed Pikes Peak in the Colorado Rockies. Every step of this 14,110-foot-high mountain was an exercise in strength and patience. Seldom could I see more than a few hundred feet in any direction, the clouds were that thick. But I kept climbing, past the timberline to where the air felt thin and my breathing became strained.

Then came the moment. One last turn, a few more strides and I was at the top. The clouds had lifted. In front of me was an endless view of land and sky like I had never seen in my life.

At that moment I could understand what the previous nine hours of climbing had meant. In that moment I was able to see where I had walked.

In the handful of days we shared together, Stanley Cheborge changed my life. Through his capacity to love and his willingness to dream, Stanley opened my heart to God. Without delivering a sermon, or leading a Bible study, *with his life* he showed me how to see each day as a new opportunity to love . . .

When I look into the eyes of the child who has had nothing to eat, will I feed her?

When I walk by the forgotten man who has no place to sleep, will I kneel down and comfort him?

But perhaps the greatest thing of all, Stanley Cheborge showed me how to walk as a follower of Jesus. And as I have tried to follow Him—even though I'll never fully understand the tragedy of a homeless Bosnian child, or a diseased Rwandan mother—I have not felt alone or worried, because I know the Lord walks with me. The evidence is all around me in the footprints of His followers:

Lilly Tesot.
Ernie Steury.
Marty and Ann Graber.
Franklin Graham.
Sylvia, my wife.
And a one-legged Kipsigis tribesman named
    Stanley Cheborge.

I look forward to the conversation he and I will have someday. On that day, there will be no shortage of time, nor things to talk about. Because on that glorious eternal day, we will stand in awe of the Lord who was leading us all along, and who will forever take delight in saying to us, "This is where we have walked."

☐ AFTERWORD ☐

A well-told story is irresistible, because it grabs your attention, your emotions, your heart. Sometimes a story is so powerful it changes everything—the way you look at the world, your life, and God. *Come Walk With Me* is one of the most inspiring books I have ever read. It is a wonderful story of what one person can accomplish in life through learning the true meaning of "faithfulness."

This amazing story is about Dr. Melvin Cheatham's encounter with a young man who impacted his life. God often reminds us of His faithfulness through His children. That is why *Come Walk With Me* speaks so directly to the heart. God used Stanley Cheborge—a Kipsigis tribesman from east Kenya—a person without wealth, status, or fame to tell *His* story.

As you read this book, you will join countless people around the world who have had a life-changing experience through this story. The operating-room drama of attempting to save the life of a young man dying of cancer in a remote African bush hospital will grip you. The knowledge that the faithful way in which Stanley lived his short life continues to lead others to faith in Jesus Christ will touch your heart.

This is a Story of Faithfulness
Because Stanley loved God, he strived to be faithful to God. Stanley loved others in the very same way God loved him—unconditionally, and with great joy.

This is a Story of Giving Your Life Away to Others
This is true freedom, to love others out of love for Christ and a desire to be faithful to Him. It clearly demonstrates that life becomes full when you begin to give it away.

Dr. Cheatham, a successful and noted neurosurgeon, shares how his life was transformed into one of service to the poor, the disadvantaged, and the needy people of the world through volunteer work with Samaritan's Purse and its medical arm, World Medical Mission. His unselfish volunteer service has inspired many. More than a colleague in ministry, more than a caring Christian brother, Mel Cheatham, a successful and noted neurosurgeon, and his wife Sylvia, have become dear and faithful friends.

This book will inspire you and motivate you to walk with the Savior.

—Franklin Graham

ABOUT THE AUTHORS

Melvin L. Cheatham, M.D. is a Clinical Professor of Neurosurgery at the University of California School of Medicine (UCLA) in Los Angeles. He is a former President of The California Association of Neurological Surgeons and of The Western Neurosurgical Society. In 1995 he received the prestigious American Association of Neurological Surgeons Humanitarian Award.

Dr. Cheatham serves on the Board of Directors of Samaritan's Purse and its relief arm, World Medical Mission.

For the past twelve years, Dr. Cheatham and his wife Sylvia have served in many short-term medical mission assignments in developing countries and in places of war around the world. In 1986 he was the first neurosurgeon ever to serve at Tenwek Mission Hospital in Kenya. At Tenwek, he treated a Kipsigis warrior named Stanley, whose steadfast faith despite terminal cancer profoundly impacted Dr. Cheatham's life and led to the writing of this book. Dr. Cheatham has written a second book, *Living a Life That Counts*, which focuses on lives he considers exemplary. It is the winner of an Angel Award for excellence in moral quality media.

Mark Cutshall is a freelance writer and speaker whose writings include material for *Focus on the Family* magazine and for several books. He has helped numerous people tell their life stories. In addition to *Come Walk With Me* he worked with Dr. Cheatham on *Living a Life That Counts*.

Mr. Cutshall is a member of the National Speakers Association and speaks several times monthly. Mark and his wife, Linda, and son, Ryan, live in Seattle, Washington.